THE COMPLETE PLAYS OF NATHANIEL HUTNER

Books by Nathaniel Hutner

Heracleitus Under Water   1988

War: A Book Of Poems   2003

The Name We Never Lose   2019

The Complete Poems of Nathaniel Hutner   2021

❧

Plays by Nathaniel Hutner

Godot Arrives

Godot Imagine Godot

Godot at Night

Godot, Alive or Dead

The President Pardons Godot

❧

Short Plays by Nathaniel Hutner

Hot Potatoes

The Fix

Keewaydin Plays

THE COMPLETE PLAYS OF NATHANIEL HUTNER

Burlington, Vermont

Individual acting copies of these plays are available from Onion River Press, 191 Bank Street, Burlington, VT 05401

Copyright © 2021 by Nathaniel Hutner

All rights reserved. No part of this publication may be reproduced, distributed, or transmitted in any form or by any means, including photocopying, recording, or other electronic or mechanical methods, without the prior written permission of the publisher, except in the case of brief quotations embodied in critical reviews and certain other noncommercial uses permitted by copyright law.

Onion River Press
191 Bank Street
Burlington, VT 05401

Names: Hutner, Nathaniel, author.
Title: The complete plays of Nathaniel Hutner / [Nathaniel Hutner].
Description: Burlington, VT: Onion River Press, 2021.
Identifiers: LCCN: 2021909907 | ISBN: 978-1-949066-83-8
Subjects: LCSH American drama--21st century. | BISAC DRAMA / General | PERFORMING ARTS / Theater / General
Classification: LCC PS3608.U865 C66 2021 | DDC 812/.6--dc23

Designed by Jenny Lyons, Middlebury VT

Printed in the United States of America

First Edition 2021

For André Vernet

CONTENTS

GODOT ARRIVES 1

GODOT AT NIGHT 129

GODOT IMAGINE GODOT 245

GODOT, ALIVE OR DEAD 363

THE PRESIDENT PARDONS GODOT 453

HOT POTATOES 543

THE FIX 557

KEEWAYDIN PLAYS 571

Godot Arrives

A Comedy

CAST OF CHARACTERS

GODOT

DANIEL: Adopted son of A & B

A & B: Two forgotten Apostles

MISS PRIMP: Royal Court Tennis Enthusiast

MISS LUST: Sex Specialist

PROFESSOR FISH: Putative Academic

TOFF I: Snob

TOFF II: Explorer

DR. GODOT: Psychiatrist, distant relative of Godot

MR. TOPS: Clinical Psychologist, Miss Lust's Assistant

POZZO & LUCKY: Representatives of the Old Order

ACT I

A
An abandoned baby!

B
Does it talk?
(Baby makes noise)

A
Evidently.

B
A foreign language. Perhaps it will be good company.

A
Other people's babies usually are.

B
Are you sure it's not ours?

A
Not very likely, though I do admit I'm fond of you.

B
I think it wants to be fed.

A
A rutabaga?

B
And two carrots?

A
Perhaps it has a strong digestion.

B
I don't think we even have water.

A
I am forecasting rain.

B
Yes, it will probably arrive with Godot.

A
It always seems to.

B
Now we are three.

A
So there's hope.

B
Yes, and a future.

A
Perhaps we should take care of our future.

B
When we were a couple, it didn't really much matter. It was mostly erections and suicide. And time.

A
I'm not fond of time.

B
It seems to be infinite, wherever you look.

A
Appalling.

B
Do you suppose it's infinite in the afterlife?

A
I don't see how anyone could stand it, even in the afterlife.

B
I would choose to be eternally present.

A
Stop with paradoxes.

B
But the baby.

A
We haven't diapers.

B
Just leave the pants off — it will pee al fresco.

A
I wonder how it feels, being abandoned.

B
Is it a he or a she?

A
He.

B
We may get in trouble with the Authorities.

A
Wait till Godot arrives.

B
He will arrange things.

A
He already has.

B
Perhaps Godot's in the afterlife by now.

A
He may be, in which case, we've got heavy-duty trucking ahead. I think a prayer might help. Let me see ... "May the grace that gives life beauty, and the love that hallows it, be with us all."

B
Ooohh.
(Baby gurgles appreciatively)

A
Would you care for a hymn?

B
Not likely.

A
A moment of meditation?

B
I'm anti-clerical.

A
A mantra's just what you want.

B
Vamoose.
(A goes offstage. B approaches child, coos over it and allows a finger to be clasped in its fist. Baby smiles. B smiles back; both baby and B are pleased. A comes back onstage and watches the other two before speaking)

A
Well, that's encouraging.

B
I know, I can't help it.

A
Paternal piety — fidus Achates.

B
We'll have to apply for custody.

A
I think we've already been elected by default.

B
Well.

A
Not that I object.

B
It would have been better if we had been sounded out. Then again, when has that ever happened? And now this one arrives, without even a dog-tag. Well, there's no one else here, so it's us or utter abandonment.

A
Don't you find him appealing?

B
Of course, only now we have to assume one more burden, another anxiety.

A
Think of the joy he will bring.

B
I can't wait.

A
And when he's grown —

B
When he's grown he'll write a nasty book about us and publish it in twelve languages.

             A

Cynic.

             B

I am a highly pragmatic person.

             A

What of the transforming power of love?

             B

You ask me that?

             A

Sorry.

             B

And what do we do when Godot arrives? How do we explain the excess baggage?

             A

Not to worry. It's for him to explain.

             B

I suppose. Do you know how to coo?

             A

I'm a little out of practice. I think I gave it up around age one. Before I start that, what should we call the little one?

             B

Hope? Faith? Charity?

             A

It's not female.

             B

How about something biblical? Or Greek?

             A

Daniel. Who slew the lion —

B
Yes. Yes …

A
It's appropriate, if you consider what we've got ahead of us.

B
One vast opportunity.

A
One big mess.

B
Call in the mops.

A
Call in — Daniel.

B
We'll never see him once he's grown.

A
If we live that long.

B
It's a good name.

A
Better than Pozzo.

B
Better than Lucky.

A
Where are those two, anyway?

B
Whipping their destiny along like a whore.

A
Now we have something better than destiny. We have hope.

B
So we have.

A
If Daniel were a girl, I would call her Hope.

B
You never know what will turn up.

A
I think it's hungry still.

B
Look, under the tree.

A
An apple!

B
Unattached.

A
Ripe.

B
I thought that tree was dead.

A
It could have been dormant.

B
Or diseased.

A
But woke up.

B
Or recovered.

A
Where there's Hope…

          B
You can turn the Universe around.

          A
Daniel seems to like it.

          B
He has teeth?

          A
No. But his mouth is functioning.

          B
I really think we need milk, in a bottle.

          A
Look!

          B
Two wonders in one day. The Delphic Oracle would have dropped a load.

          A
Remember the bard: the milk…

          B
Of human kindness.

          A
You make me weep.

          B
Me too.

          A
It's almost too much to bear.

          B
We'll survive, even this.

          A
Daniel is sucking like an old pro.

B
He's in practice.

A
I've read about this somewhere…

B
Oscar Wilde?

A
The cloak room at Victoria Station!

B
Miss Prism!

A
Shall we call him Earnest?

B
Of course. It's highly appropriate, especially if we are to be the parents.

A
With or without the A?

B
With — after all, that's the point of it.

A
Our own Earnest!

B
Do we burp him now?

A
Yes. You go first.
(Baby burps after a few bounces on B's shoulder)

B
I think he got up more than just air.

A
I'll clean you. There.

B
Now for a nap, Daniel Earnest.

A
Quite adorable. Think. Now we have someone to live for besides ourselves!

B
Very gratifying.

A
Not that I was tiring of you. Still, after the passage of some time, a change in the human landscape can be welcome.

B
I quite agree.

A
Oh.

B
Listen to him laugh.

A
I was a smiling baby.

B
What happened?

A
Those who were insecure thought I was laughing at them and fell away. All but you.

B
I understood.

A
Yes.

B
There he goes again. It's positively heartening.

A
More useful than a scowl.

B
It makes for good company.

A
And optimism as to future developments.

B
Why do you laugh?

A
I'm inspired. Who's here?

MISS PRIMP
Miss Primp. Can you tell me the way to the court?

B
Royal or sporting?

A
Why both, of course.

(B ?)

MISS PRIMP
The Royal Tennis Court. There are only fifteen in the world, and I have played on them all.

A
Did you win your match?

MISS PRIMP
That is not what matters. I play to bolster my opinion of myself. Royal tennis props me up. It's a tonic.

A
Oh.

MISS PRIMP
Yes. And the exercise is vigorous. I adore vigor.

A
That's not the only thing you adore.

MISS PRIMP
Quite right. I also adore Mr. Godot.

A
Have you seen him?

MISS PRIMP
Not quite. But I have heard volumes. Volumes. The philosophers would say I know him by acquaintance — by hearsay. I do. I know him intimately by hearsay. And there is very much to know.

B
We expect him.

MISS PRIMP
Mr. Godot?

B
Yes. Presently.

MISS PRIMP
How unfortunate. I have a game scheduled for three o'clock which I cannot miss. Do give him my sincere regrets.

B
Yes. We shall.

MISS PRIMP
Well, then, good-bye.

B
Goodbye.

A
Goodbye.

B
I wonder if she knows how to read a ouija board?

A
Not likely.

B
Have you ever wished to know your future?

A
Not likely.

B
Would sort of deflate everything, eh? Destroy your sense of freedom, make you a victim of determinism?

A
What?

B
Well, everything would happen according to plan. You would choose what you knew you would choose, and so on. There would be no room for the unexpected.

A
I ask myself — how would Godot feel about this?

B
Not very happy, I am sure.

A
Everything foreordained — even for him.

B
Appalling.

A
Well, that is not the case with us. Not yet.

B
No. We must try to preserve our ignorance. Have you ever heard of Miss Lust?

A
Who?

B
Miss Lust. We have an appointment with her today.

A
Oh, the one that produces vibrations.

B
Yes.

A
Well, good heavens, there she is!

MISS LUST
I am Miss Lust.

A
You know Godot?

MISS LUST
Yes, we are intimately acquainted

B
You?

MISS LUST
Certainly. Well, I should say we have been intimately connected in parts.

A
Good heavens.

MISS LUST
Precisely. He's very knowledgeable and is always willing to learn. I have taught him many things.

B
Many things?

MISS LUST
Of course. No one knows all that I know about, well, lust. Unless I instruct them. Mr. Godot, in fact, was a very apt pupil. He enjoyed learning.

A
Very apt?

MISS LUST
Yes.

B
Well, this is news.

MISS LUST
I could give you details, but that would be kiss and tell. Ask him when you see him. He is not ashamed to talk of me, of us. He is very kind.

B
And where are you off to?

MISS LUST
To play tennis.

A
Royal tennis?

MISS LUST
Yes.

A
I think you have a partner just ahead of you.

MISS LUST
Either gender will do.
(A and B: raised eyebrows)

      A
I wonder if there is a Mr. Lust.

      B
You tell me.
(A and B exchange glances)

      A
Do you suppose?

      B
But it was so long ago.

      A
Do you still feel that way, even a little?

      B
Sometimes. I have really never been able to get over you.

      A
How handsome we were.

      B
Yes.

      A
How much in love.

      B
Yes.

      A
We thought — well, we never thought of us, here.

      B
No. But we lived.

      A
And still do, to a degree.

      B
Look: Daniel's smiling.

                A

It will be much different for him than for us.

                B

Externally. Inside, I think the feelings are the same whatever way you turn out.

                A

Another visitor!

                B

What is this place, Piccadilly Circus?

            PROFESSOR FISH

I am Professor Fish.

                A

A man of parts!

            PROFESSOR FISH

Yes. A Bachelor of Parts, a Master of Ceremonies, and Doctor of Verbal Disturbances.

                B

Quite a combination.

            PROFESSOR FISH

I am versatile.

                B

Have you any idea why we are here?

            PROFESSOR FISH

No.

                B

To pass the time.

                A

You seem to have passed your time quite well.

PROFESSOR FISH
I would really like to be an actor.

B
Why the degrees?

PROFESSOR FISH
I did so well in kindergarten, I just kept going.

A
Acting's not for everyone.

B
Don't be so sure.

PROFESSOR FISH
I lecture poorly, my students detest me in tutorial, and my research is renowned throughout the world. Not that anybody will be reading it fifty years from now.

A
In the meantime, your students abandon the fields you teach because you turn them off.

PROFESSOR FISH
I hadn't thought of that.

B
Professors rarely do.

A
If you ask me, it's all a racket anyway — like most professions. The pupils' parents pay the fees, the pupils drink beer and learn how to fornicate, and after four years they collect their diplomas and go out into the world, where they cash them in and fornicate some more.

PROFESSOR FISH
Cash them in?

   A
Yes. They cash in their diplomas for the rest of their lives, particularly if the diploma is from a highly-rated institution. A diploma bordered in crimson gives you a lot of mileage, not only at work, but also in casual conversation at cocktail parties.

   B
I never speak about mine.

   A
I know. You don't believe in labels.

   PROFESSOR FISH
Oh!

   B
It's true. With all your degrees, you're just another professor to me, covered with labels.

   A
And there are plenty of professors about, even bordered with crimson.

   PROFESSOR FISH
Oh!

   B
Don't worry, the rest of us don't know the important questions — or answers — any better than you do. You just pretend to. The fact is, you're a professor because you can bear to read three books a week — and even that pace you don't keep up past age thirty. Well, I can read, too, but I would much rather spend my time outside, with our tree, our baby —

   A
And me.

   B
And Miss Primp and Miss Lust and — surprise — <u>you</u>.

PROFESSOR FISH
I manipulate words, not people.

B
It can come to the same thing. Look at me, a poet manqué, who can turn most situations to account, often without knowing it.

PROFESSOR FISH
Peculiar.

B
Not really. All you have to do is stick around and keep your eyes open. Then you either practice or you're practiced upon.

PROFESSOR FISH
I seem to be the latter.

B
Touché.

A
He really isn't as cynical as he makes out. He just wishes he was innocent again, and since he's not, he gets angry and indulges himself by pretending he's wicked. It's a common psychological game. All wind, below decks.

B
You're too true.

A
You will be, too, if you want.

B
(To PROFESSOR FISH)
It is very likely that you would know more if you knew less.

A
Drop the books.

B
Take up bar-hopping.

A
Bridge.

B
Baseball.

A
Acting.

PROFESSOR FISH
Ah!

B
Learn to improvise.

A
Tell dirty stories.

B
Collect bottle caps.

A
You see?

PROFESSOR FISH
When do I start?

B
Right now. There is a Royal Tennis Court just off there to the left. You will like it.

PROFESSOR FISH
Thank you so much, both of you! I really didn't care for Plotinus anyway.

A
Not at all.

B
Not at all.

A
Just remember James Joyce.

PROFESSOR FISH
How so?

A
He thought he would fool the Professors, but the Professors fooled him.

PROFESSOR FISH
How do you mean?

A
Who reads Finnegans Wake?

PROFESSOR FISH
Yes.

B
Off with you!

A
How's the little one?

B
Taking a snooze.

A
Ahhh!

B
Not you. You're not a professor yet. And he wanted to be an actor.

A
He was.

B
Your wit is irremediable.

A
You are too.

B
Do you know what time it is?

A
I would say twoish. Of course, it's hard to say precisely: the sun has got unreliable in the modern era, what with Relativity, and the Waste Land. We are all adrift in an empty room, and so on.

B
I wouldn't have minded being Caesar. All that solid accomplishment.

A
I think the Christians ruined everything: their ideal is self-abnegation. If you have any scruples at all, success ceases to be sweet.

B
Well, here we are.

A
But we're not Christian.

B
We must have been at one point, or we wouldn't be here.

A
And consider chastity.

B
I never did, even when I was alone.

A
More's the point. It just is not human nature to be chaste;

and those who are generally have no choice. They pretend to despise what they secretly crave.

    B

A few have no cravings, and for them there is nothing to give up.

    A

Like turtle soup.

    B

For Lent.

    A

How about the Confessional?

    B

Talk about rackets. The Church makes a thousand impossible demands on you. Surprise — you fall into sin. So then you feel guilty and voilà, see the Father Confessor, who makes you whole again. Then back to square one.

    A

Sounds like emotional blackmail.

    B

Bingo!

    A

Is there another way?

    B

You had best consult your imagination.

    A

But —

    B

I know it's work, but try.

A
But I can't answer any of the important questions.

B
That's a beginning.

A
I proceed from there?

B
Correct.

A
And create my life as I go along —

B
Like an artist of the soul.

A
I shall try to grow.

B
Even to the end.

A
Look!

B
One more weary voyager.

TOFF I
Halloo!

B
A prototypical toff.

A
Of what is he the fruition?

B
We shall see.

TOFF I
Is either of you a Jew?

B
If not by birth, then certainly in spirit.

TOFF I
I am a pillar of society, I reside in a very exclusive neighborhood, I own a Rolls, I know Politicians to whom I make generous gifts, I am a vestryman of my church, I speak French and adore the Opera, I sit on fashionable Boards, my children play with the sons and daughters of famous publishers, artists, investment bankers, lawyers, clergy; I even play polo when invited and can shoot pheasant; I have a country-house, a wife that rides a horse, my reputation is of the highest order — and I went to Harvard.

B
Call no man happy until he is safe in the grave.

TOFF I
I am very far from it.

B
You live perpetually at its edge —

A
Death is a very good guide in life.

B
It keeps you on your toes.

TOFF I
How morbid.

B
I guarantee it.

A
It is inevitable.

B
And if you don't learn it here, there is plenty of space elsewhere for you to learn it in.

A
You will only be finding yourself.

TOFF I
Nonsense. I have told you who I am.
(A and B exchange glances)

TOFF I
(Continued)
I am Mr. Toff, and I command respect from all who know me. Perhaps I require more from life than others. That is my privilege.

B
Well said.

A
But watch out for that edge.

TOFF I
Nonsense. I must go. I am late for a luncheon appointment.

A
Goodbye.

B
Goodbye.

TOFF I
Good riddance.

A
Do I see his twin approaching?

B
I believe so.

    A
Same clothes, same tilt, same complexion.

    B
The nose is smaller.

    A
Not aquiline.

    B
My grandfather had an aquiline nose — he was very distinguished. He believed in co-operatives.

    TOFF II
Hello. A bit gusty.

    A
Yes.

    TOFF II
You're not cold?

    A
Well, yes, somewhat.

    TOFF II
Here, it fits you better than it did me.

    A
Oh!

    B
Good heavens, a manneqin.

    A
No. Just a man.

    TOFF II
I am Sir William Toff II.

    B
I am B.

> A

I am A.

> TOFF II

I have been to Ethiopia, the Sudan, the Outer Hebrides, and so on. But I always come home.

> A

You must tell us what the world is like, at least the parts we don't already know.

> TOFF II

Well, curiously enough, the people are much the same. It is their circumstances that change.

> A

But that is true even if you stay at home.

> TOFF II

Indeed.

> A

Then why did you go?

> TOFF II

Like the Roman soldier in Lucretius, I was trying to get away from myself.

> B

You'll manage soon enough — none of us is immortal.

> A

Yes. We just wait and watch.

> TOFF II

I like activity.

> B

But not action.

A
I meant to ask: did you ever find yourself?

TOFF II
With you, here, I feel for the first time that I may look inside and not be appalled.

A
Oh, we've been appalled.

B
It wears off after a bit.

A
You find out soon enough that, as you said, everyone's pretty much the same.

B
You just have more scruples than usual. That is all.

TOFF II
I shall need a new occupation.

A
How do you stand financially?

TOFF II
Dead broke.

B
A person of your station?

TOFF II
Travel is not the best way to make money, and I am a younger son of a younger son. My father was an Egyptian civil servant.

A
Do you have any unique talents?

TOFF II
I can smell out the truth about people.

    B
Hurrah.

    TOFF II
That's the advantage of traveling. You see everything.

    B
And —

    A
Shh.

    TOFF II
And I can turn a phrase.

    A
A poet!

    B
He has no occupation, he has no money, he's perspicuous about people and he can turn a phrase. A natural. Have you ever written verse?

    TOFF II
Well…

    A
You needn't be shy with us.

    TOFF II
If you like, I'll recite one of my better (!) efforts. Ready? It's a Comment on War:

    Now Reason's drowned
    Amidst a flood of fools fearing fools,
    And Folly's crowned
    With witless words, our witless minds to rule.

    A
Bravo.

B
Very good for an initiate. Could we anoint you Poet Laureate? Everyone should have a title; titles grease the wheels of Society.

TOFF II
But I haven't any money.

B
Most of Society doesn't either, until they get married.

TOFF II
I have no desire to get married.

A
That's all right, we love you already.

B
You really are a poet.

TOFF II
Of life, and now of words.

B
More than words.

A
We people may be similar in as many ways as you have seen, but few of us claim poetry as our purpose in life.

TOFF II
I have very little to lose.

B
And we have much to gain.

A
Remember, in this field volume does not count: one poem, truly written, admits you to the fellowship of the word.

B
And you can never be tossed out.

           A
As for your personal life —
(B coughs)
           TOFF II
Meeting you two is quite an experience.

           A
And we're not even in the Outer Hebrides.

           B
We're close.

           A
Do you have another poem?

           TOFF II
Well, my repertoire is limited, but I think I can do one more:

    Blue leaf leave me,
    Blue metal on the lawn,
    The long way down
    Is new to me
    Though not new to all.
    White fire of dew
    On leaves, white steel
    Of dew, turn to ice
    On fallen trees,
    Turn to ice in fall.

           A
Definitely Poet Laureate material. We, the Committee of Two, nominate you. Any opposed? You are elected.

           TOFF II
That's new.

           A
We do what we can.

B
Much more.

TOFF II
You make me weep.

A
A toff — and you weep?

TOFF II
I walk into the desert and find friends, a home and an occupation, as well as myself.

A
Would you care for a rutabaga?

B
Carrots?

A
And we'll have water as soon as it rains.

B
Yes.

TOFF II
I have seen men die, but I have never seen them so true.

A
Well, now you have.

B
Try to repeat the experience.

A
We've forgotten Daniel!

B
He was sleeping.

A
Would you care to meet — our child?

TOFF II
Is this an example of Parthenogenesis?

A
I don't know. But we have adopted an orphan.

B
Yes, even though our union has never been solemnized, Fate has made us parents. You're beaming.

A
Yes. It is a great pleasure to be loved by the young. It was something I didn't expect.

TOFF II
Most true gifts are.

B
(To TOFF II)
I can learn from you.

A
(To B)
You already are.

TOFF II
May I hold him — is it Daniel?

A
Oh, yes.

B
And his middle name is Earnest.

A
With an "A".

B
It's our personal plaisanterie.

TOFF II
Daniel. Well.

A
If you look deeply into your own child, you will find a good part of yourself.

TOFF II
Ohhh.

A
How's Daniel?

TOFF II
Bubbly. He looks like both his Daddies. It's odd: an orphan.

A
And we've had apples, too.

B
And many visitors. Even here.

A
Near the Outer Hebrides.

B
On the heath.
We weep, like you. We've always liked company. And we don't talk politics. — But that's something else.

TOFF II
Well, here is Daniel. I must go on.

A
If you care for Royal Tennis, just turn left over there. You'll find some people playing already. I'm told it's quite an exclusive game. As Poet Laureate you'll fit right in. You can be a spectator. Action should always have a home in reflection.

B
And vice versa.

A
Goodbye.

B
Goodbye.

TOFF II
Ciao.

A
Would anyone care to take a photograph?

B
I could send one to my mother.

A
Where is she?

B
Waiting for Godot, last I heard.

A
Even photographs lie.

B
Pretty depressing.

A
How's Daniel?

B
O.K.

A
I wonder when he'll begin?

B
To lie?

      A
Uh-huh.

      B
Perhaps we should put him in training.

      A
I'm not aware that we ever lied.

      B
We spared ourselves — for this...
(Looks around)

      A
I hope Daniel takes after us in that.

      B
Good heavens!

      A
What?

      B
Look! Another apple!

      A
It seems we inhabit the Garden of Eden.

      B
We could sell cider. Ouch.

      A
I shall make a pie for Daniel. I shall use Mrs. Cray's recipe.

      B
Mrs. Cray?

      A
My nursemaid. Before we met.

      B
I'm glad to hear it, happy to have company.

A
Do you suppose it's Mackintosh?

B
Northern Spy?

A
Red Empire?

B
Delicious?

A
That's odd. There seem to be different varieties — from the same tree.

B
There you have it.

A
Plucked from the mud.

DR. GODOT
I am Dr. Godot, Analyst-in-Chief of the Magdalene Mental Mercyseat.

B
Sounds grand.

A
Any relation —

DR. GODOT
Of course. We are fourth cousins twelve times removed.

B
Ah, a voice in the choir. I believe we know each other.

DR. GODOT
(Examining him carefully)
Yes, you may have been a patient. I am an authority on

masochism. I remember that you had a curious compulsion — which we won't discuss — as well as paranoid tendencies.

    B

The world being what it is...

    DR. GODOT

Yes, you suffered enormously.

    A

I am glad to hear it.
(B and DR. GODOT look at A)

    A

(Continued)

It makes us that much closer, one to the other. It is something we have in common, besides love.

    DR. GODOT

Yes, pain is a paradox. And logicians know that a paradox implies any proposition.

    A

Proposition? Let's not be vulgar.

    B

Darling.

    DR. GODOT

I have come to administer a follow-up examination on you.

    B

Thirty years later?

    DR. GODOT

There were some minor funding problems.

    B

You mean it took you thirty years to pay off the Department of Mental Health?

DR. GODOT
That and the paperwork. And what with committee meetings, grant applications and so forth, I have only now found the time to pursue one of my most illuminating cases.

B
Well, here I am…

DR. GODOT
What do you live on?

B
Water. When it rains.

DR. GODOT
Any children?

B
I have adopted an orphan, with A here.

DR. GODOT
Are you on medication?

B
Not that I know.

DR. GODOT
Any loss of memory?

B
Voluntary or involuntary?

DR. GODOT
Involuntary.

B
I remember what bothers me.

DR. GODOT
I'll put down involuntary. Do you still have any paranoid phantasies?

        B
Only if they have a basis in fact.

        DR. GODOT
Married?
(B gestures to A)

        DR. GODOT
(Continued)
Oh. Any plans to alter your marital status?

        B
I'd rather die first.
(A smiles)

        DR. GODOT
Any problems with insomnia?

        B
Only when the moon is full and there are no clouds.

        DR. GODOT
Please count to ten.
(B does so)

        DR. GODOT
(Continued)
Now please count backwards from ten.
(B balks)

        A
He never was a math whiz.

        DR. GODOT
All right. One more question: are your emotions overwhelming, available but under control, or absent?

        B
They are available and for the most part I control them. When I am provoked, they control me.

DR. GODOT
Not bad.

B
Is that it?

DR. GODOT
For now. Thank you.
(To A)
Thank you.
(DR. GODOT exits)

A
I guess he's not into tennis.

B
Too many things on his mind. 30 years???

A
Leave it. If he comes back, we can worry ourselves then. And please don't fill me in — your past is not pertinent here. We must tend to the young one.

B
One day he'll have a happy past. It's our gift to him.

A
Yes.

GODOT
Lively time.

A
Who?

B
What was that?

GODOT
I say, you've had a more than usually lively day.

A
Are you planning to contribute?

GODOT
Indeed. If you will allow me.

B
You sure are starched.

GODOT
I'm a bit out of date. There. I usually try to suit my surroundings.

B
Oh. I'm B, this is A.

GODOT
Enchanté.

B
And you.

A
Yes.

GODOT
Call me Max.

A
Nothing else?

GODOT
Not for the moment.

A
Well, it's simple.

B
Max?

GODOT
Yes.

B
You come from these parts?

GODOT
Amongst others. Tell me, have you been waiting long?

A
Since we were born.

B
Approximately two millennia.

GODOT
Your patience becomes you.

B
Indeed.

GODOT
And — for whom do you wait?

A
Oh, Godot.

GODOT
Friend, acquaintance?

B
Savior. Who are you, the Prince of Perplexity?

GODOT
And this Godot, who is he?

A
We're not certain. But we know that —

B
We know nothing.

GODOT
Evidently.

A
We would like to know something, as a matter of course.

GODOT
Well, everything is worth something, and some things may be worth everything.

B
Touché.
(Grins)

A
May I quote you?

GODOT
Of course.

A
You are easy, aren't you?

GODOT
I try to please.

B
Good luck.

A
You remind me of Cupid.

GODOT
That has been said of me before.

A
Do you suppose Cupid was allowed a lover of his own?

GODOT
Highly unlikely.

A
Why do you say that?

GODOT
He would have to be partial to one over the rest — for him an impossible situation.

A
And so he goes loveless?

GODOT
I am afraid that is the case.

A
To be fair to everyone, he must love them all equally?

GODOT
Right.

A
It's a neat trick.

GODOT
I've always thought a God, Roman or otherwise, should be allowed at least one personal attachment. But then gods are highly impersonal, especially Modern gods.

A
If I did without B, I would be nowhere.

GODOT
Yes.

A
And Daniel.

GODOT
Is he a God?

A
Not yet.

GODOT
(Pained expression)
And do you know why you wait?

B
We are out of work. Temporarily.

A
In the autumn we pick apples.

GODOT
By then it's too late.

A
Excuse me?

GODOT
I say, how long do people live around here? I mean, what is the normal span of life?

A
It all depends on diet.

B
Rutabaga.

A
Carrots.

GODOT
And you two?

A
It's hard to predict.

B
If you like your occupation, you may go on indefinitely.
(GODOT: pained expression)

A
Of course, retirement is generally required.

B
Then we drop like stones.

A
Boredom.

B
Emptiness

A
Loneliness.

B
Anguish in the face of the unknown.

A
That is not new.

B
No.

A
But we all suffer, one way or another.

GODOT
And who arranged things this way?

A
Well, Mr. Godot is supposed to arrive soon, and I'm sure he'll give you an answer.

GODOT
And Mr. Godot, where does he come from?

A
(Laughs)
That's a good one!

B
He doesn't come, he goes.

GODOT
How will you know him, if he comes?

A
Oh, he's very distinctive. Very noticeable.

B
Yes, we have eyewitness accounts of him that are very reliable.

A
And he has a son, whom some know at first-hand.

GODOT
Any distinctive features for Monsieur Godot?

A
Well, he speaks daggers and his eyes are like fire. He is usually dressed in red and carries a scale in which to weigh souls.

GODOT
Souls?

A
Oh, yes, he is a master of souls; some he sends to Heaven, and the rest go to Hell.

GODOT
Forever?

B
Yes. Forever.

GODOT
I don't think I care much for this Godot. And what is Hell?

A
I'm not quite sure, but I do know you can never get out of it.

GODOT
(Pained expression)
For all eternity?

B
Indeed.

GODOT
Well, that much I knew. And so you are waiting.

B
Yes. Care to join us?

GODOT
Not right now, thank you.

A
You look a little depressed.

GODOT
Thinking of eternity always fatigues me.

A
Why? the possibilities are limitless.

GODOT
Precisely.

(A ?)

GODOT
I prefer something a bit better defined.

B
Like mortality.

GODOT
I've tried that too.

B
Not your bag?

GODOT
Well, death was very relaxing, but there was not much to it.

A
Can't you find a compromise?

GODOT
That is why I am here. I have come to consult you two.

A
Three.

GODOT
Three?

A
Don't forget Daniel.

GODOT
Oh! How handsome he is. And which one of you —

B
Both.

GODOT
(?)
Oh. I didn't realize you could…

A
It's an orphan.

B
It's adopted.

A
But we love him more than ourselves.
(GODOT is somewhat pained)

B
Oh, love is in short supply. I'm sure the Authorities would let you adopt, if you want.

GODOT
I'm afraid that's in the same category as marriage — for me.

A
What are you allowed to do?

GODOT
Pretty much what I want. Right now I have arranged things so that I could consult you about the possibility of a compromise?

B
Compromise?

GODOT
Yes. Between mortality and the infinite. For the deuce of me, I cannot come up with an answer. You two (three) spend what time you have face to face with both.

A
Well, we hope to be granted life eternal, you know, when…

GODOT
And you really find the idea of eternal life attractive?

A
I don't suppose it would be much different than what we have now — except we could look forward to its continuing indefinitely into the future.

(Looks puzzled — A and B look around themselves, at themselves)

GODOT
You see what I mean?

A & B
I think so.

GODOT
Do you think that perhaps Mr. Godot has an answer?

A
Very likely.

B
I am convinced of it.

GODOT
Well, please let me know what he says. I must be off. Do let me know —

A
Bye.

B
No orphans for him?

A
Apparently not. Certainly not one like ours.

B
How is he?

A
He's asleep. The soul of innocence. I wish I could sleep as he does. I vaguely remember that I did once. An axe! Shall I wound you?

B
Not likely.

A
I shall have to get back into shape. But we have no wood.

B
What about the tree?

A
It would improve the view.

B
But we need apples — for Daniel.

A
Right you are.

B
Even in small numbers.

A
Yes. Well, I shall wave it about. That will make potential aggressors think twice.

B
You will just aggravate them.

A
Nonsense. We require —

B
Look, please get rid of that thing. Otherwise you may amputate your nose. Then you would have to move to L.A.

A
Why?

B
That's where the plastic surgeons are — I have a grandfather who has just enjoyed his fifth face-lift.

A
I wonder if I need one.

B
There are other things you need far more.

A
I know I'm vain.

B
Well, we have no mirrors, so you can't encourage yourself. We don't even have a reflecting pool.

A
We have Daniel. We can see ourselves in him.

B
No comment.

A

What put you in a bad mood?

B

I am running out of patience.

A

With whom?

B

Life.

A

Would you like an apple?

B

They give you the trots if you eat too many.

A

Then you need cheese.

B

This is ridiculous. All we do is talk.

A

I enjoy conversation.

B

I want action.

A

Sometimes we act, too.

B

Ach!

A

It beats working.

B

That is utterly false. Not-working, not-doing is the hardest work in the world. Every single person I have ever known who has tried it either went mad, became an alcoholic or committed suicide. I do not refer to Eastern Yogis — they, at least, can meditate.

    A

We can't leave here, we've got to wait for Godot.

    B

Take a look at Daniel. We can wait for him. Imagine him at eighteen — he will find a girl, go to university — he might even thank us for our pains as parents.

    A

Not likely. Did you ever thank your father?

    B

Certainly not. I told him his mistakes.

    A

What about your mother?

    B

She made no mistakes.

    A

That's a mistake.

    B

Yes.

    A

Let us be loving but fallible.

    B

All right. Can you plan these things ahead?

    A

Probably not.

    B

What if he likes one of us more than the other?

A
That's normal, though most religious people I have known say it isn't Christian.

B
(??)
Are we Christians?

A
Well, Unitarians.

B
What on earth is that?

A
One of the more obscure heresies.

B
God knows I've been a heretic. And I am certainly not a Christian. Nobody I know is, even the Christians. Though if they realized that, and tried to improve —

A
We'd have more company.

B
Money!

A
What?

B
I've found money in my shoe!

A
So that's where the pain came from.

B
I've been limping for twenty years! And all the doctors said it was psychological!

    A
They were right.
    B
Yes. Well, now that we are rich, I propose we eat something. A chocolate shake. For two.
    A
For three.
    B
Oh. Damn!
    A
Yes — we have to save it for Daniel — his shots, his teeth, his clothes — his education.
    B
My education didn't cost me anything, except some pain.
    A
Daniel must have a proper upbringing.
    B
Yes.
    A
B, our tree has no leaves.
    B
It has apples.
    A
But why no leaves?
    B
It is old. Leaves are green, and green is the color of youth. Our tree is not young. What it has to offer now is the fruit of its age. And that is what we have to live on.
   "All that lives must dies,
   Passing through nature to eternity."

    A
Oooh — you've got back your memory!

    B
A few tidbits.

    A
That was wonderful. Who said it?

    B
I forget.

    A
Well, I shall try to remember it, too. Two heads are better than one.

    B
Shakespeare.

    A
Don't tease. You always were impressive with your quotes. I remember when you had half the Odyssey down, in Greek. No one knew what you were saying, but the sounds were very melodious. Professor Parry would have been happy.

    B
Who?

    A
Milman. Milman Parry.

    B
I'll let that one pass.

(A shrugs)

    B
I wonder if Homer made a buck out of poetry. If he did, he was the last.

                    A
You can still write for pleasure.

                    B
What else <u>could</u> I write for? You used to call me perspicuous, and I was. Poets are proud to see, even more than to write. Well, look around for a while, and you're headed for lunacy or suicide: the occupational hazards of the poet. In self-defense I tried to close my eyes. What happens? I dream! Which is worse than being awake. So I returned to my verse, eyes open. As you may see, my muse and myself are still collaborating.

                    A
I always admired your courage.

                    B
Thank you. We have to make choices.
(They look at each other. They are very much in love)

                    B
(Continued)
   What time is it?

                    A
Close to sunset.

                    B
Miss Primp!

                MISS PRIMP
Yes.

                    B
How was your game?

                MISS PRIMP
Superbly invigorating. I adore vigor. Mens sana in corpore sano: Mind and physique in good trim. You should try it. It quite cleans out the brain. And the participants are always

respectable. As a rule, Royal Court Tennis is an infallible test of social acceptability.

B
The cream may float on top, but so does the scum.

A
B!

MISS PRIMP
You said something?

A
He's on a diet of water and apples — no energy for exercise.

MISS PRIMP
How unfortunate. I hope his case is not terminal.

B
Mortality usually is.

A
B!

MISS PRIMP
Oh, has Mr. Godot made an appearance?

A
Not yet.

B
We think he may have forgotten the time.

A
It's very easy to do. Especially in fine weather.

MISS PRIMP
Well don't let him keep you. You must set a time limit, and if he doesn't show up, proceed without him. Otherwise you will be immobilized indefinitely.

A
Waiting is not a treat.

B
But we have hope.

A
And a future.

MISS PRIMP
That's nice. Well, goodbye. No doubt we shall meet again.

B
If the fates are kind.

A
Yes.

MISS PRIMP
Yes.

B
So she goes. I wonder if Miss Lust can be far behind.

A
Aha!

MISS LUST
Oh!

(B laughs)

MISS LUST
How delightful to see you again. You know I like handsome men, and both of you are perfectly adorable — just like my pet schnauzer, Ding-a-ling. In fact, I can tell, you all have many characteristics in common. You're alternately anxious and irritable, especially if dinner is not on time; you like to laugh (Ding-a-ling has a charming little whimper, like this…); and you are all gentle, even when it goes against your mood. As you

know, when the atmosphere is heavy, it is my opportunity to provide some warmth, even heat, to those in need.

B
How did she ever get such a bad press?

A
I believe it all began with St. Augustine.

B
Pray, dear God in Heaven, let me be good, but not yet.

MISS LUST
Is sex not good?

B
There are those who would have us think so. But, of course, they haven't met you.

MISS LUST
Oh!

B
Next time we see one, we'll give you a ring.

MISS LUST
A new challenge!

B
I'm certain you'll do yourself credit.

MISS LUST
I must be off — I have an appointment with Mr. Godot.
(B !)

MISS LUST
We won't be long — just some evangelizing on behalf of mortality's bright spots. Then he's yours.
(She goes off)

B
Life's ironies are sometimes quite precious.

A
Where would we be without her?

B
That's obvious.

A
You and I, what would Mr. Godot say?

B
We are all children of Providence.

A
We are all children of God.

B
We are beginning to sound like the Archbishop of Canterbury.

A
Quite likely. Two more apples.

B
It must be getting on toward dinner.

A
Daniel dines first.

B
May I?
(B takes DANIEL and administers food)

A
Time for evacuation. Watch out!

B
That was a bit close. Of course, I've been hit with worse.

A
Let's leave that alone.

B
Righto.

A
What do you think Godot is like?

B
More revolutionary than the Apocalypse, more reactionary than Death, perfectly persuasive, eternally present, invariably true, merciful and righteous, semi-comic and unitary.

A
Well. I could use that resumé.

B
You wouldn't want it.

A
But he's whatever he wants to be.

B
That doesn't make him any other than what he is.

A
Everybody and everything!

B
You're highly amusing.

A
Oh, come on, can't you let him alone?

B
What's the point? He's the only one like him there is, or can be.

A
He needs a girl.

B
My foot.

        A
He's lonely.

        B
Very good.

        A
Only he can keep himself company. Only he can be his equal.

        B
Ugh.

        A
Miss Lust! You're back!

        MISS LUST
I always come back. Several times, at the least, even in one day.

        B
More news of Godot?

        MISS LUST
I hear he has been jettisoning a good part of his powers. He wishes to be like us. A trial run. Omniscience and omnipotence have their deficiencies.

        A
So we think.

        MISS LUST
That is all. Goodbye.

        B
That was quick.

        A
She makes a great Evangelical.

        B
Unlike us.

A
Just because you can't raise the dead.

B
I'd rather join them.

A
Only a little further patience is required.

B
It seems that we have all of the hard questions and not one of the easy answers.

A
It follows that we should stick with what we know and perfect our own lives as far as we can.

B
That is an honorable occupation.

A
It might even be fun.

B
Stop! You make me giddy.

A
Radical change can do that.

B
And here comes a radical change.

A
Professor, you look beat.

PROFESSOR FISH
I thought teaching was tough. Try Royal Court Tennis with Miss Lust — or Miss Primp. It will make you wary of Feminists. They could take over the planet, the two of them.

            B
I thought they had.

            A
They've just kept it a secret.

            PROFESSOR FISH
It's damnable.

            B
Pleasure damnable?

            A
At heart he's a puritan. That's what makes him such a doctrinaire left-winger.

            PROFESSOR FISH
Why do I tolerate your abuse?

            A
Because it's true.

            B
Think about what we say. It will change you.

            A
You need it.

            B
You don't need degrees and books and pimply pupils, thirty year-old lecture notes and tweed jackets no one would put on a corpse. You need imagination, humor, compassion, vision, character, courage, a musical ear, a voice that charms, eyes that are open, grace of body, depth of soul, a refined intellect and a profound and real tolerance for all whom you may encounter in this life.

            A
And that means that you do not take pupils - or anyone else - under your wing. You give them your wings, if that is what

they require, and wish them a fruitful journey.

    B

It is call generosity of spirit - and that is the spirit that moves the world.

    A

Look inside yourself — you will find it.

    B

And you will feel it. It is the one gift besides life - that really has value.

    PROFESSOR FISH

I feel completely inadequate.

    B

A very good place to start. Giving up the garbage is very hard, and making a present of the rest is truly frightening.

    PROFESSOR FISH

I must advance.

    A

That's it.

    B

Good luck.

    PROFESSOR FISH

It seems you will set me free.

(He goes off)

(TOFF I appears. A and B both turn their backs to him and find some activity to keep them diverted until he is almost offstage, at which time B speaks)

    B

How many friends do you have?

TOFF I
Two. And they are just like me.

B
Any enemies?
(TOFF I does not answer)

B
I don't suppose you know why?

TOFF I
Why what?

B
Why you have made yourself the Enemy of the People?

TOFF I
They are common. I am not.

B
In what way?

TOFF I
I have money, breeding and social position.

B
With two friends?

TOFF I
I could have more.

B
No doubt. I guess the money and breeding are what make you uncommon.

TOFF I
Yes. And my style.
(B winces)

B
So these are the things in life you most value.

               TOFF I
Of course.

               B
Do you have a heart?

               TOFF I
Of course.

               B
Has it been touched?
(TOFF I looks confused and a little unnerved)

               B
Well?

               TOFF I
I guess not.

               B
Will you move over here for just a second - I want to look at your forehead.
(TOFF I moves to B. B lightly grazes TOFF's forehead with the back of his hand. TOFF does not move. Then B begins to caress the back of TOFF's head, stroking his hair. TOFF begins to cry)

               B
You've never felt that before.

               TOFF I
No.

               B
Do you know what it is called?

               TOFF I
No.

               B
It is called compassion. You feel it as much as the next fellow.

Perhaps more.
(TOFF I sobs. B wraps his arms around TOFF I and holds him tightly)

B
I double as a mother in real life, too.
(TOFF I smiles between his tears)

B
Your tears become you much better than your airs.
(TOFF I smiles again and stops crying)

B
Feel better?

TOFF I
(Shyly)
Yes.

B
Welcome to humanity. We're not such a dreadful lot, even the common ones.

TOFF I
I expect even my type is not uncommon.

B
You're not exactly scarce.

TOFF I
No. Who is that?
(TOFF II enters)

B
That's your soul-mate. He is all the things you haven't been.
(To TOFF II)
Hello!

TOFF II
Greetings. I see we have another Toff to handle.

B
He's manageable once you touch him.

TOFF II
I'm willing.
(Embraces TOFF I)

TOFF I
Oh, I think I may melt.

B
That's one way of putting it.

A
A love-match, like ours.

TOFF II
Pardon us. We need some peace in which to breathe.

B
Of course. Love grows best in repose.

A
Shall we repose?

B
It's not yet time for us.

A
The doctor's back.

B
Fourth cousin, twelve times removed?

A
Uh-huh.

DR. GODOT
Your case has at last been correctly diagnosed.

B
Pray, tell.

DR. GODOT
Bipolar with paranoid affect.

B
Well?

DR. GODOT
At least that's what we were looking at thirty years ago.

B
Without seeing it.

DR. GODOT
Science does advance.

B
So do I.

DR. GODOT
Yes.

B
Any more up-to-the-minute bulletins?

DR. GODOT
From today's observation, I would say you are entirely cured. In fact, you are not only normal, you're unusually gifted, in mind, body and spirit. It is a pleasure, a treat, to know you.

B
I can't believe it.

A
What?

B
That he says these things.

A
They're true.

B
Why did no one ever say them before?

A
I suppose they thought you knew, and that if they told you how they saw you, they would spoil what was there.

B
And you?

A
You have always known how I felt. I was not exactly disinterested. So you discounted what I said, and rightly, I guess.

B
I'm beginning to feel human.

A
It's not so bad.

B
That's what I've always maintained.

A
Well, here we are.

DR. GODOT
That's my cue. Stay well. Flourish. You have many friends who love you, some of them even more than themselves.

A
They're only returning what they receive.

B
Goodbye.
(Tears pour down his cheeks)

A
The bearer of good news. When did the intelligentsia ever give him a fair shake?

B
In their childhood, which they prolonged indefinitely by trying to grow up.

A
There seems to be one person left on the dance-card: a Mr. C. Or perhaps Mr. G. I can't quite make it out.

B
He'll pass the time.

GODOT
Hello. I'm not late, am I?

B
We haven't even begun waiting.

GODOT
Any news from Mr. Godot?

A
He hasn't arrived.

B
There is still time.

GODOT
Yes.

A
We have spent the time meanwhile —

B
Discovering ourselves.

GODOT
That is helpful.

A
You are Mr. G., aren't you -

B
Or Mr. C?

GODOT
Sometimes one, sometimes the other: it depends on my digestion.

B
Then you have an alias?

GODOT
Yes, for photo opportunities. I don't want to give myself away. Think what would happen to my fans.

A
Yes, baseball lives on images.

GODOT
Daniel requires attention.

B
Let me.

GODOT
Religion lives on images too, few of them accurate.

A
B and I are agnostics - we don't know.

B
And we don't want to.

A
Certainly we do. After all, what else is there to wait for besides knowledge?

GODOT
Why don't you do something?

B
Then we might find out something.

A
Horrors.

GODOT
You have started with that baby. Please continue with yourselves.

A
Double horrors.

GODOT
Not at all. It will hurt - and that is how you know you are in transit between ignorance -

A
And bliss.

GODOT
If that is what you want.

A
Are you related to Mr. Godot?

GODOT
In a way. I am his shadow.

B
Jung.

GODOT
Yes.

A
(?)
But then, where is he?

GODOT
He has come - you spoke with him.

A
We did?

B
Without knowing it.

A
Then what are you doing here?

GODOT
I'm the herald, only I come after the fact.

B
A damp squib.

GODOT
If you like.

A
Who is Jung?

B
A Swiss crackpot with too many wives.

A
Bertrand Russell had five wives, and many mistresses.

B
He needed the exercise.

A
We're of a different persuasion.

B
For these many years.

A
We have always had one another.

B
Without a ceremony, even.

A
Or the blessing of the Church.

B
Or a lawyer's fee.

GODOT
Then what binds you together is to be found within you. That is good.

A
We have had our bad times.

B
Mostly on account of very attractive adventurers: they're secretly envious of us.

A
They don't know how we do it.

GODOT
But you do it anyway: bravo!

B
Modern society seems to be based on the maxim that all rules are made to be broken.

A
And they have been -

B
And where did that leave us??

A
So here we are —

B
Making up rules —

A
For ourselves.

B
If anyone else cares to participate...
(Laughs)

    A
You know, laughter is not entirely mad.

    B
No, nor the wisdom of a fool.

    A
It's getting late.

    B
It has been for some time.

    A
Perhaps he is like us.

    B
Godot?

    A
Yes: he only admits the mistakes he doesn't make.

    B
He doesn't make mistakes, he just advertises them.

    A
Why?

    B
I think he needs to feel evil without being evil.

    A
Are you sure he hasn't simply gone overboard?

    B
Circumstances would seem to suggest it.

    A
How do we rectify things?

    B
Copulate.

    A
Thanks.

    B
I'm not kidding. It's the almost universal bid for pleasure and immortality.

    A
What about the offspring?

    B
They are a mirror to the character of their parents: they adopt, willy-nilly, most of their parents' faults and none of their virtues.

    A
Daniel has virtues of his own.

    B
And we can appreciate them only because we are not his natural parents. His natural parents would be threatened by them and throw him out.

    A
They have.

    B
Daniel's precocious.

    GODOT
Still waiting?

    A
Look at the apples!

    B
We have a monopoly of the tree of knowledge!

    A
I could make a pie — or applesauce, even.

GODOT
Don't eat them all at once.

A
Flowers!

B
Music!

A
Rock music!

B
Jazz!

GODOT
Gershwin!

A
I smell a roast of Virginia ham.

B
It's raining.
(A and B look at GODOT)

B
Are you Godot?

GODOT
Only you know that.

A
But it has rained.

GODOT
"The rain it raineth every day."

B
Indeed.

A
Il pleut dans mon coeur.

    B
Comme il pleut dans la ville.

    A
Good heavens, a rainbow — a triple rainbow.

    GODOT
    Thrice three makes nine,
    Swears the sage to the blind,
    The heart's ahead,
    The head's behind.

    A
Do we know you?

    GODOT
As well as yourselves.

    A
The face —

    GODOT
It is not faces that count, nor names.

    A
Are you Godot?

    GODOT
No more so than you.

    B
A real sphinx.

    GODOT
I cannot lie.

    A
What a sweet odor.

    B
Gardenias.

GODOT
A very delicate bloom.

A
It is beginning to make sense.

B
How?

A
Well, we are Godot. We have been waiting for ourselves.

B
What next?

A
We act.

B
How?

GODOT
You choose.

ACT II

A
Well, that was tasty.

B
Better than water and apples.

A
Our little tree stood up remarkably well for the hanging.

B
It's good practice. You never know who may need hanging.

A
I'm not used to being a cannibal.

B
Some people make it a matter of faith, though it doesn't keep the from starving.

A
So much for Godot.
(Burps)
Very light and digestible.

B
Yes. I expect things to improve here on out.

A
Do you think our diet will make us divine?

B
I don't notice any change.

A
It reminds me of Zeus and Cronus.

B
The same old story. If we were more numerous, we could stage Titus Andronicus. It's very true to life.

A
Are we being wicked?

B
Yes.

A
Rather fun.

B
It's a change.

A
Do you think we'll be punished?

B
We already have been. Now we're supplying a sufficient reason.

A
Oh.

B
It's a case of everything in moderation. We don't want to be too good. It would spoil the balance in our lives. And evil offers broad new opportunities for action and knowledge.

A
I don't like it.

B
What's wrong?

A
It doesn't suit my idea of myself.

B
That can be altered.

A
I liked myself better before we ate Godot. And besides, it sets a bad example for Daniel.

B
Oh.

A
Daniel is the light in my life. I don't want the light to go out.
(B is silent. A starts to cry)

B
I suppose we could hang ourselves, though it wouldn't do Daniel much good.

A
Who will forgive us?

B
That's the one thing we can't do for ourselves.

GODOT
Having a picnic?
(A looks up and smiles. B appears astonished)

GODOT
Pray, don't let me interrupt.

A
Please do.

B
I thought we ate you.

GODOT
You forgot that I am Godot. And one of my ground rules is: only I can do away with myself. In any event, you both looked pretty hungry, not to say desperate.

A
We need to be absolved.

                B
(Not so contrite)
   Yes.

             GODOT
   Granted. Anything else I can do?

                A
   I love you.

             GODOT
(Smiles)
   Thank you very much. How about Scrooge?

                A
   He wants to improve the world.
(General silence)

                B
   We hate the world at large largely because we hate ourselves.

             GODOT
   No joke?
(B smiles wanly. A smiles)

             GODOT
   I cannot be responsible for you. If you want a guide or exemplar, I am available. And there are other people available, too.

                B
   We don't know them.

             GODOT
   Yes, you do.

A
Are they left-wing, like us?

GODOT
Oh, the confines humans make for their minds! They are neither left nor right, nor anything in between. They are individuals, each one of them unique and self-sufficient. They take others as they come, and help them when they can. They are not afraid of their feelings. Their love lives are well-regulated: they are neither possessive nor promiscuous, nor jealous, nor cruel. Above all, they wish to give. And what they receive in return - never looked for - is my original gift to them: life.

(A and B are silent)

GODOT
I could go on, but moralizing is only talk. What you need is a good kick in the arse.

(He chases A and B around stage. They all fall down, panting)
(MISS LUST appears)

GODOT
Miss Lust, we need you. Desperately.

MISS LUST
(To B)
When was the last time you tried to copulate?

B
The Battle of Agincourt. I was violently attracted to a page-boy on the opposing side.

GODOT
Well?

B
Oh, we consummated our passion. He subsequently died in medias res — like a dog.

(General silence)

GODOT
(To A)
And you?

A
(To B)
I never knew about that one.
(B looks miserable)

A
Well, I have not fornicated since 1066. I just tease — and if things get dicey, I retreat rapidly into paranoia. In short, I am afraid.

GODOT
Miss Lust?

MISS LUST
May I quote Dido? Non ignara mali, miseris succurere disco. Or: "They called her Flower because she had been through the mill." Dear boys — you both have more company than you could imagine. That is what really keeps me busy. It is not the satisfied customer that comes back to me. It is the people with problems. And the problems are as numerous as the people. That is one reason why I like my job.

B
The other reason is that you like the people.

MISS LUST
Very good.
(B looks little less miserable)

MISS LUST
Now you two like men. So do I, but I am not a man. I have therefore invited a friend to join us — Mr. Tops. I am quite sure you will like each other.

(She whistles. A young man 27-30 in appearance, enters)
Tops, these are my friends, A and B.
(They shake hands)

MISS LUST

Well, if you need help of a kind I can supply, please whistle.
(She exits)

MR. TOPS

First of all, you know that the cure for sexual problems is sex.
(A and B look a bit startled)

MR. TOPS

If you will move over here, I think I can help out. It shouldn't take long.
(They move to a remote corner of the stage)

GODOT

Busy, busy, busy.
(Lights down. Eighteen years pass. Lights up. Everyone is just as before, except the baby, who has disappeared. Enter a young man, eighteen, handsome in every way: DANIEL)

GODOT

Daniel!

DANIEL

Yes?

GODOT

We have been waiting.

DANIEL

For me?

GODOT

Who else?

DANIEL

You flatter me.

GODOT
Not at all, not at all.

DANIEL
Have you any idea where my fathers went?

GODOT
They're finishing up a seminar on sex.

DANIEL
I thought sex came naturally. Like learning how to swim.

GODOT
Some people drown.

DANIEL
Oh.

GODOT
Not you.

DANIEL
No. I like girls and they seem to like me. I have no complaints.

GODOT
Girls don't threaten you?

DANIEL
Certainly not. We understand each other.

GODOT
What about your fathers?

DANIEL
I have yet to understand them. They never talk about themselves. For all I know, they haven't had sex in 573 years. In fact, I find it difficult to think of my fathers in bed, copulating.

GODOT
They do too.

DANIEL
Oh, so that's why they're having a seminar?

GODOT
Yes. These days it's called therapy.

DANIEL
I hope it helps.

GODOT
We all do.

DANIEL
Who is that?

GODOT
Miss Primp.

MISS PRIMP
Halloooo!

DANIEL
Hello.

GODOT
Hello. Back for tennis?

MISS PRIMP
I've given it up.

GODOT
Indeed.

MISS PRIMP
I now spend my time in India, helping the starving millions. But it is very difficult. The lower orders seem to like dying better than anything else. And it makes my job very hard. I am always thinking of myself as a kind of high-class undertaker. I can see that life for most of them is not worth much, but I am trying to alter that. I must help them find some good reason to live.

GODOT
It is not easy.

MISS PRIMP
No, but it is better than Royal Court Tennis. For the first time in aeons, I feel useful. And that makes me happy. I know the war will be long, and I shall not outlive it, but what I can do, I shall do. And that is that.

GODOT
You seem to have gained weight.

MISS PRIMP
I got married.

DANIEL
You still look fetching.

MISS PRIMP
Thank you. I suppose I can attract in a matronly way. I do not complain, neither does my husband.

DANIEL
Would you like a game of tennis?

MISS PRIMP
Thank you, but no. You are young. Try it for yourself. It may be somewhat rarefied, but that just means that you should approach it in a proper state of mind. It is not an engine for evil — certainly no more than anything else we do. Think of it as one of those deservedly obscure pleasures that pop up in most people's paths once or twice in a lifetime. Take advantage of it. That is what it is for.

DANIEL
Thank you. Thank you indeed.

GODOT
Me too.

(MISS PRIMP exits)

DANIEL
I hear laughter.

(GODOT smiles)

DANIEL
I think they've finished their therapy.

A
18 years!

B
Considering how long we've been here, with our problems, 18 years are not long.

A
I feel as though I've been inoculated.

(GODOT laughs)

B
Now what?

GODOT
I must move on to other puzzles. If you need help, remember: Mr. Tops is tops.

A
We will.

B
Cheerio.

DANIEL
I am reconnoitering.

A
Around us?

DANIEL
Yes, I have to. I'm eighteen and inexperienced. You two are practically Methuselahs.

B
Charming.

A
Shhh.

DANIEL
My life has not been simple.

(B rolls eyes)

B
You have much to look forward to…

DANIEL
I'm not sure I like the example you have set.

A
We've been in therapy for eighteen years.

DANIEL
Precisely. You've neglected me.

B
Good heavens.

A
But Daniel, now we are prepared to help you.

DANIEL
I am old enough to take care of myself.

B

(To A)
I told you. He'll write an exposé.

A
We'll be celebrities.

B
(Looking at audience)
Seems we may have got there already.
(A is looking at audience, squeals in delight)

DANIEL
None of this alters the fact that I have been neglected.

B
What next?

DANIEL
I need an allowance.

B
(Laughs)
We've made one rutabaga and two carrots stretch quite far. See if you can do the same.

DANIEL
But all my friends have cars, beer, girls…

B
You earn yours.

DANIEL
I haven't ever had any of those things except girls.

B
We love you.
(This does not make much of an impression on DANIEL)

A
We are willing to help as we can, with what we know.
(DANIEL exits abruptly)

B
Anyone for tennis?

A
Do you think he'll come back?

B
Yes. With a pair of adopted parents, one of them female. We'll get over it. We have been preoccupied. I suppose we neglected him.

A
We must have: look how he turned out.

B
What I want to know is who looked after him for 18 years?

A
Miss Lust.

B
Yeoww. The high priestess of the Hedonists.

A
She always seemed nice to me.

B
Niether of us has seen her in action.

A
Well, there's nothing we can do now.

B
Our one son, gone the way of all flesh.

A
He'll recover. We did. We all grow old.

B
True.

A
Look — the skies are the color of blood.

B
We've missed dinner.

A
We talk too much.

B
No, we just concentrate on what we say.

A
And time goes by.

B
To bed! Exeunt.
(Lights up. Next morning)

GODOT
I resign.

A
Impossible.

GODOT
Nonsense. I am Godot and I resign.

B
Well? Any results?

A
Nothing noticeable.
(To GODOT)
You're still here. Intact.

GODOT
You see: No one has ever given *me* a choice.

A
You could try death again. Warmed over even.

GODOT
Once was enough.

B
Here we are, the three of us.

A
The music is nice.

B
The gardenias are definitely a plus.

GODOT
And you have each other.

B
And progeny.

A
Why not invite Miss Lust to drinks?

GODOT
I've exhausted that one.

B
Isn't lust a renewable resource?

GODOT
If you're doomed to eternity, everything becomes a renewable resource — even imagination. Sometimes I think the Universe has played a great joke on us all, including me — that it will not last forever. That it is, in fact, not indefinitely renewable.

A
You're supposed to know.

GODOT
I know.

B
It's certainly possible. Isn't there a law of thermodynamics?

GODOT
Of course! That's it. The whole machine is running down, and me with it. I knew I came to consult the right people. Brilliant.

      B
Well?

      A
Well what?

      B
How do we spend the time that's left?

      A
You could start by blowing your nose. It's drippy.

    GODOT
It's odd.

      A
What's odd?

    GODOT
I begin to feel mortal.

      B
Welcome to the inner sanctum.

      A
Or the outer limits.

    GODOT
You're amused.

      B
Even Godot comes a cropper.

      A
But where did we all begin?

    GODOT
All out of nothing, and all back to nothing.

            A
Not even dust?

            GODOT
No. Nothing.

            A
What is nothing?

            B
That one I wouldn't touch for an eternity with Miss Lust.

            A
Or Mr. Tops.
(GODOT shrugs to say 'I don't know')

            GODOT
Nothing can be said about Nothing.

            B
If nothing can be said about it, it must be something.

            A
Touché.

            GODOT
Or nothing.

            B
Enough. Conventional conversation cannot survive on such an insubstantial plane. Let's talk about something.
(Silence)
(The TOFFS enter)

            B
Salvation.

            TOFF I
We are returning the favor.

TOFF II
We have never been so happy.

TOFF I
You have rescued both of us.

TOFF II
And you have allowed us to see what we are.

B
That you did on your own, though I thank you for the compliment.

TOFF II
We think we may adopt.

B
I can provide you with an eighteen year old.

TOFF I
We would prefer to begin with an infant.

A
That's what we did.

B
(Glumly)
Yes.

GODOT
An eighteen year old can certainly be infantile.

A
It is not easy to be a parent.

B
Yes.

TOFF II
Do you think it could be arranged?

GODOT
Without doubt. Come with me.
(GODOT, TOFF I and TOFF II exit)

B
I would have preferred a chocolate shake.

A
What?

B
When I found the money in my shoe — we might as well have spent it on ourselves.

A
In a way, we did.

(B ?)

A
We lived through our child.

B
But he grew up.

A
Precisely. And he is not now what we anticipated.

B
I suppose he'll grow some more.

A
If we are all lucky.

B
And you and I may grow too.

A
It is not impossible.

B
In fact, he may show us something about life.

A
It is certainly possible.

B
Remember Mr. Tops.

A
I do.

B
I love you.

A
Yes. We are a satisfactory couple.

B
Much more.

A
Yes.

B
Ohhhh.

PROFESSOR FISH
The salmon are biting. Oh, excuse me.

B
Not at all.

A
The salmon are biting?

PROFESSOR FISH
Yes.

B
In Vermont?

PROFESSOR FISH
Oh. They must be trout.

B
My favorite.

A
(To PROFESSOR FISH)
He's a disciple of Julia Child.

B
There is nothing better for any meal or any time than a lightly poached rainbow trout freshly caught in a Vermont stream. The scenery itself is worth the trouble.

PROFESSOR FISH
Oh, it's no trouble, at least for me. That is why I have taken it up. I like it.

A
It suits you.

PROFESSOR FISH
I know, my name.

A
No. It is a contemplative activity and it is outdoors. It turns your attention away from yourself and fixes it on something far more grand and engrossing.

PROFESSOR FISH
You mean Nature?

A
Yes.

PROFESSOR FISH
That's how I feel. I have even become acquainted with the names of trees, flowers, ferns, mosses, butterflies and birds. The outdoors has much to offer.

B
What about your career?

PROFESSOR FISH
I intend to make a career of Nature.

B
Can you support yourself?

PROFESSOR FISH
Not at first, I suppose. But with time I shall find a way. After all, this is something I truly love to do. It's the first time I have put my life on the line.

B
Very good.

PROFESSOR FISH
I think so.

A
No more Plotinus?

PROFESSOR FISH
No.

A
Maiden-hair ferns are certainly more beautiful.

PROFESSOR FISH
I am off. Do visit if you are in the neighborhood. I shall show you my Japanese tea-garden. The water talks as it falls. And I have learned to listen.
(He goes off)

B
Well, that's a change.
(A smile)

B
Look!

A
Pozzo -

           B
And Lucky.
(Enter POZZO with his rope coiled over one shoulder. LUCKY has another rope on his shoulder. They both appear in blue stripe business suits)
           A
We haven't seen you in years.
           POZZO
We are modifying our behaviours.
(A !)
           LUCKY
I was tired of masochism.
           POZZO
I was tired of my self-indulgence, amongst other things.
           LUCKY
So I stood up. It hurt.
           POZZO
His back was out of joint - but he stood up.
           LUCKY
Yes. And then I spoke.
           POZZO
I was astounded.
           LUCKY
So was I.
           POZZO
He said -
           LUCKY
I said, "I would like something to read."

POZZO
So I gave him the Times.

LUCKY
I had no idea there were other people - other lives.

POZZO
Other than ours.

LUCKY
It floored me.
(POZZO nods his head)

LUCKY
And then I read <u>about</u> the other people. They seemed to be doing things.

POZZO
It was novel.

LUCKY
So I thought - why not me?

POZZO
But that is only half the story.

B
What's your half?

POZZO
As soon as Lucky stood up, I sat down. It was delightful. I had never thought there could be relief, but there was. And then as Lucky became human, I began to realize that I could, too. I thought, "Why not cooperate? We shall go into business for the two of us and divvy up the work and the rewards - as our talents allow." So we did.

LUCKY
We have made a success of it, too.

B
So I see.

A
Why do you keep the ropes?

POZZO
As a reminder of what in our past to avoid.

LUCKY
We have also taken up rock climbing.

B
In Vermont?

POZZO
How did you know?

B
It's known for its rocks.

A
I was born there!

B
Yes, I know.
(To POZZO and LUCKY)
Good luck with the business.

LUCKY
Thank you.

POZZO
If you ever need a dollar -

LUCKY
We are expanding. We even hire the disabled - they love to show what they can do.
(B looks at A meaningfully)

POZZO
Good-bye.

LUCKY
Good-bye.
(They go off)

B
That was unexpected.

A
No comment.

B
I guess we're alone now.

A
What about Godot?

B
He's probably hanging around.

A
But he said he had trimmed his wings.

B
They'll grow back.

A
And Daniel?

B
I expect an occasional visit, wife, grandchildren.

A
We're in our golden years now.

B
They're an improvement - thanks to everyone -

A
And us!

B
Well, we did put some effort into changing. But I still have no desire to do a lot of radical nonsense. Just living is radical enough.

A
Where does the time go?

B
I thought we had figured that one out - from Nothing to Nothing.

A
There is very much in between.

B
Yes, as much as anyone, including Godot, could want. Quote the Bard -

A
Ripeness is all.

B
We are ripe. We may be a little rotten.

A
It is very quiet.

B
Our tree is asleep.

A
After all those apples.

B
I have the trots.
(Leaves the stage running)

A
Au revoir.
(A putters around till B returns)

B
That was close.

A
Have some cheese.
(They smile)

B
I used to play the piano.

A
Badly.

B
It drove everyone up the wall.

A
It was kind of you to let them down.

B
It's my specialty. Up and down.

A
Do you realize that we're very near our two thousandth anniversary?

B
So soon?

A
What we have seen!

B
Beats this place.

A
Nonsense. It's time we rested. We can savor our memories.

B
Why ask for trouble?

A
I thought we had reformed you.

B
You did. I just bounced back. Everything has its natural shape - and I have mine. Please respect it. If it comes to trouble, that is my concern.

A
You are very prickly this evening.

B
I want you.

A
Well, that was easy. Now?

B
Yes, while there's still some light. I hate dining in the dark.

A
Ooohh!

(B growls. Lights fade. Night)
(Another morning)

A
Do you like the gardenias?

B
At a distance.

A
What?

B
They're very sweet, and sweet things invariably end up costing you something.

A
Like a rotten tooth.

B
Or a broken heart.

A
I feel ambitious.

B
Maybe today you'll do something.

A
I always used to think ambition unseemly - from a radical point of view.

B
How absurd. The radical are more overblown than everyone else combined. That is why they are radical.

A
Then ambition is all right?

B
It depends whether you want to live on rutabagas and carrots.

A
I could use an Egg McMuffin occasionally.

B
And I am still on the track of a chocolate shake.

A
Perhaps you could form a business.

B
A going concern?

A
Yes! Yes! We could market our concern. Mr. Tops showed us all his tricks. They are not patented. And Miss lUst said there's plenty of demand. And we have apples to eat till we accumulate some capital. In fact, our apples are our capital.

B
Metaphorically speaking.

A
Yes. Oooh - I'm feeling more ambitious than ever.

B
Don't you need a degree to do this sort of thing?

A
(Deflated but not defeated)
I shall get one. Perhaps Professor Fish could help.

B
I think it would be more realistic to go into apples. We have enough. Besides, at our age we're supposed to decline gracefully into the grave.

A
Well I won't. I wish to be of use till the end.

B
Here's Daniel. If it's money you want, look in your shoe.

DANIEL
(Mystified)
I came to say good-bye.

B
How considerate.

A
Oh, Daniel, we apologize if we have made mistakes.

B
We hope you do not compound them.
(DANIEL looks startled)

A
We wanted to give you a happy past.
(DANIEL appears sad, along with A and B, especially A)

      A

We did not intend to fail. It just feel out that way. We would like to make peace. We would even offer you what's left of our lives to help you through all that lies hidden ahead of you. We love you.

      B

Indeed we do.

(DANIEL is totally disarmed)

      A

We all know what we have seen. The problem is how to turn it to account.

      B

If you leave, go quietly…

(Silence)

     DANIEL

I'm thinking.

      B

(To A)

For God's sake, don't tell him to <u>do</u> something.

     DANIEL

Do we have to stay near the Outer Hebrides?

      A

I've always adored London.

      B

Or Paris.

     DANIEL

We'll be destitute to start.

      B

I think we can manage that one.

A
We always have.

DANIEL
Agreed.

A
Agreed.

B
Agreed.
(Music: Spring, from Vivaldi's Four Seasons)

GODOT
(Enters)
I hear you three are off to London.

B
How did you know?

GODOT
I am all ears. May I come too? With you?

A
Of course.

B
As long as you don't pull rank.

GODOT
I wouldn't dare.

A
Of course not.

DANIEL
Otherwise you would give yourself away.
(B smiles)

DANIEL
Be subtle.

GODOT
I shall be invisible. Metaphorically speaking.

B
Do we have a plan of action?
(Enter POZZO and LUCKY)

A
We are blessed.
(To POZZO and LUCKY)
You said your enterprise was expanding. Could we fill in the empty spaces?

POZZO
Of course, eh, Lucky?

LUCKY
No problem.
(To GODOT)
You too?

GODOT
Why not?

LUCKY
No joke?

GODOT
Of course not. Even I need an occupation of some kind. And what you offer is highly novel for me. I look forward to working with you.

A
Me, too.

DANIEL
Let's make it unanimous.
(They do)

      A
Look, our tree! It's wilting.

      B
It weeps for thee.

      A
Where shall we ever find another?

      B
All we need to do is plant a seed.

      A
Which you have!

      B
In abundance.

      DANIEL
Off!

(They all leave. TOFF II appears and reads)

      TOFF II
Keep to poverty, and a poet's candid soul, the love you give your friend, I'll give my foe and not be poor thereby.

(TOFF I enters and reads)

      TOFF I
…Who loves most loves secretly…

-FINIS-

Godot At Night
൭

A Comedy

CAST OF CHARACTERS

FATHER ANSELM: A monk, about 40

GODOT

DANIEL: Adopted son of A & B

A & B: The two forgotten Apostles

MISS PRIMP: Fiancée of Professor Fish

MISS LUST: Educator

PROFESSOR FISH: Retired Academic

TOFF 1: Spouse of Toff 2

TOFF 2: Spouse of Toff 1

DR. GODOT: Psychiatrist and remote cousin of Godot

TOPS: Assistant to Miss Lust

POZZO & LUCKY: Politically ambitious deadbeats

MR. PEUCH (LATER PEACH): Merger Specialist

WAITER

ACT I

SCENE 1

A
I figured Godot would bring rain, but not the deluge.

B
Has it been forty days and forty nights?

A
More.

B
History is overtaking us.

A
We shall have to add a new chapter to the Pentateuch.

B
More.

A
In the beginning, there was a beginning –

B
And a middle –

A
And an end.
(A farts)

    B
Save that for the end.

    A
There is one end, but many beginnings.

    B
I am feeling sick to my stomach.

    A
You are a wonder and a joy. Does my presence help alleviate the pain?

    B
Without you I would be nowhere.

    A
Yes. It is hard to put pain in its place.

    B
I don't remember – why are we here?

    A
Our enterprise failed.

    B
Pozzo and Lucky?

    A
They cooked the books and decamped with the cash.

    B
And our livelihood.

    A
So much for day-laborers.

    B
So much for the desk-executive.

    A
We'll survive.

B
We'll see. And Daniel?

A
You don't remember?
(B is silent in his anguish)
Daniel died
(B is still silent)

A
(Continued)
He collaborated with Pozzo and Lucky. They killed him and dressed it up as a suicide. I believe if we visit a certain meat-packing plant...
(They both break down)
(MISS LUST appears)

MISS LUST
(To herself)
Job suffered less than these two.
(We see tears on her cheeks)
They have lost their one son; and for them, he was the wealth of the world. Tragedy herself is not so cruel.

B
Ah, Aphrodite!
(Still choked up)

MISS LUST
I give you my heart.

B
Too late.
(Pause)

A
To everything there is an end. Even misery must end.

B
I hope death lives up to its reputation.

MISS LUST
What has become of Godot?

A
He's on holiday.

MISS LUST
He died again?

A
Yes, several times. He abandoned his identity, and without it he was nothing.

B
How long do we have to wait this time? I am tired of waiting.

A
I think this time he is waiting for us.

B
Where?

A
I think on the other side of life.

B
Good heavens.
(Pause. A looks at B)

A
It seems we have all failed to redeem ourselves.

MISS LUST
Nonsense. You have simply been victimized.

B
Well, I am prepared to act.
(Surprise)

A
What do you propose?

B
My old stand-by: suicide.

MISS LUST
I am not ready. I mean, I have so many more people to help.

A
Up to you.

B
Ready?

A
Ready.
(A and B kill themselves – the manner of death is left up to those involved)

MISS LUST
I wish I inspired such devotion... I might as well try it myself. I have had enough love, and without love, I am free to be responsible.
(MISS LUST kills herself)

PROF. FISH
(Entering, sees bodies)
Oh! A and B; and Miss Lust! Dead! A threesome! What on earth shall we do without Miss Lust? She is irreplaceable.

MISS PRIMP
(Arriving)
I shall miss A and B much more. They were faithful – even to themselves.

PROF. FISH
Well, they have all finally arrived.
(Ghosts of A and B appear)

    A
We don't seem to be very much mourned.

    B
I hope there is someone besides us at our funeral.

    A
We are not Winston Churchill.

    B
Thank you.

    A
We may have been simple, but we were not ordinary.

    B
We had our beguiling moments.

    A
Sustenance is no longer in doubt.

    B
We are even free to fly.
(They float up a bit and wiggle their wings – newly visible)

    A
We need practice

    B
I never thought my role in the afterlife would be to impersonate Peter Pan.

    A
Look, they cannot see or hear us!

    B
Just as well. Primp was a pill.

    A
And Fish, even in Nature, was a bit of a ding-a-ling. Now that we are translated, I wonder if we can find Daniel.

(A and B wander offstage)
(DR. GODOT enters)

MISS PRIMP

Death is not very attractive, at least this side of it.

DR. GODOT

It was not meant to be.

MISS PRIMP

I wonder why?

DR. GODOT

It beats me.

MISS PRIMP

Perhaps it's because death is the door to bliss. Every major religion, except the Hindus, acts as though the opposite were true.

DR. GODOT

We wouldn't want everyone to know, if it were true. It would become fashionable.

MISS PRIMP

Right: humanity requires an education, and acquaintance with as much pain as possible. Once that is done, and the memory of it firmly engraved upon the brain, then we can proceed to Paradise and enjoy ourselves. Pain will be only a memory, and memory will be a preventative.

DR. GODOT

I'm sold.
(They kill themselves)
(Enter TOFF 1 and TOFF 2)

TOFF 1

A massacre!

TOFF 2
They are not fools.

TOFF 1
Reminds me of a board meeting I once attended. Is suicide really the next fashion?

TOFF 2
If so, I hope it lasts.

TOFF 1
I have always been curious…

TOFF 2
Me, too.

TOFF 1
Shall we?
(They kill themselves)
(PROFESSOR FISH and MR. TOPS enter)

PROF. FISH
Ah, the ultimate cure.

TOPS
Let us hope so. I am tired of cures.

PROF. FISH
There will be no one left.

TOPS
No one to screw.

PROF. FISH
No one to love.

TOPS
No friends, no enemies.
(They exchange glances)

TOPS
(Continued)
Then, at last, the world —

PROF. FISH
— will be at Peace.

TOPS
The fish will ponder their subaqueous guilt.

PROF. FISH
And the trout will grow thick as thorns.

TOPS
The hummingbird will be able to hear its own tune.

PROF. FISH
Enough. Let us do Mother Nature a favor.
(They kill themselves)
(POZZO and LUCKY enter)

POZZO
We escaped.

LUCKY
At last.

POZZO
Damnation!

LUCKY
What?

POZZO
There is no one left for us to tyrannize over.

LUCKY
We have money.

POZZO
What do we spend it on? Coffins?

LUCKY
But money can buy you anything. Love, sex, an altered face, an altered name, whole caravans of sweets from the East, pornography, psychoanalysis, speech-writers, political office, paintings by the famous, paintings of the famous, fame, even a Greek Temple for a tomb. We should be happy. Now everything belongs to us.

POZZO
Sit, slave.
(LUCKY trembles and sits)
(LUCKY is once more mute)
(Out come the ropes, only this time there are two)

POZZO
Forward, cur!
(They gradually move offstage)
(BLACKOUT)

SCENE 2 - HEAVEN

A
Well. Our suffering is finally paying off.

B
This chocolate shake is exquisite.

A
And there's a choice: we can have strawberry as well.

B
Variety beats tedium. Have you noticed, I'm not such a crab any more.

A
You are well rid of life, so let's not dwell on it

B
Do you think we may run into Godot here?

DR. GODOT
Here I am!

A
Oh. The relative.

B
I thought you might have ended up in the downstairs department.

DR. GODOT
Oh, no. Everyone comes here. Even those who love life.

A
But they never suffered.

DR. GODOT
That was not their fault.

A
Oh.

B
You mean we sat around for two thousand years of pain and some twerp who lucked out in life gets the same reward?

A
I think we had better discuss this with Mr. Godot. I may ask for a refund, or a replay, or whatever.

B
Well, I'm happy to be here. Let us make the most of our opportunity.

DR. GODOT
But it isn't exclusive.

B
I don't think that's quite the right response.

DR. GODOT
Oh?

B
No. There is no such thing as social rank here. We are all dead. Why should we continue to torture each other? That is what life is for. You go through life to get it out of your system. Perhaps you should return and work on it some more.

DR. GODOT
Return?

B
Yes. It can be arranged.

DR. GODOT
I think I prefer death to life.

B
Good. Then don't muck it up.

A
Or you may find yourself reincarnated as an ass.
(DR. GODOT wilts)

A
(Continued)
Death has its rules, you know.

DR. GODOT
How do I find out what they are?

B
By breaking them.

A
It's quite a responsibility.

B
But you're up to it.
(MISS LUST enters)

A
Oh, Miss Lust – you don't look like a tart anymore.

MISS LUST
Not here. There is no sex allowed. And love is out the window. Here we do not live for pleasure, or pain, as the case may be. We are generous with our time, and enjoy each other's company. The variety of angelic types is staggering Everyone has a history. It is amazing. And they actually talk about their histories.

A
In life, that was something to avoid.

MISS LUST
Here there is nothing left for them to lose.

> B

I am beginning to wonder whether life had any attractions at all.

> A

I think we were getting strung along.

> MISS LUST

Well, death seems adequate – even the blue haired ladies are amusing themselves. You should see their hair-do's: straight out of 1955.

> B

I love it.

> MISS LUST

Not only that, the supply of new angels, each with a fresh new history, is inexhaustible. I was sure that procreation had a purpose, and now I know what it was: to make angels!

> A

And we were so afraid of death.

> MISS LUST

With good cause. There is no sex in heaven, and if there is no sex in heaven, there has to be sex on earth. Otherwise, we would sooner or later run out of things to say to one another, and there would be no new angels to supply the deficiency. In fact, without life, there would be no one in heaven at all –

> B

– except Godot.

> ALL

Ahh!

> DR. GODOT

And love keeps the whole machine in gear.

MISS LUST
It is Mr. Godot who has set it all up.

A
Daniel!

DANIEL
Hooray for Godot! He told me you had arrived.

B
Yes. Here, everyone has arrived, even the aristocrats.

A
We must take care –

MISS LUST
Of anyone who happens along. It is a good way to make new and lasting friends.

B
You're the expert.

MISS LUST
(Smiles happily)
Thank you!

B
(Smiles back)
You see: here a barb has no point.

A
Are they available for export?

B
Barbs?

DANIEL
Shall we try business again?

B
I prefer listening to Rimsky-Korsakov.

DANIEL
He is certainly pleasant to know. I ran into him on the way over. Of course, I had no idea who he was, until I asked. He was very civilized, without being blasé. And he has a very handsome beard.

A
Do you think we might run into Shakespeare?

DANIEL
I asked Rimsky-Korsakov about that. He says Shakespeare is very much in demand. And the bard is more closely related to Godot than our Doctor here. If you are really keen, I think I could arrange a meeting, but you would have to hold up your end of the conversation.

A
(Looking less interested)
Well, I don't suppose I should intrude...

B
It can wait.
(Looking at A)

MISS LUST
Someone's missing.

DANIEL
Pozzo and Lucky.

DR. GODOT
They've decided to take over the world. In fact, they have taken over the world.

A
I feel sorry for the world.
(General silence)

DANIEL
I don't suppose…

B
Oh, no. Just when we begin to unwind.

DANIEL
If we go back, we can unwind there too.

A
What's the point?

DANIEL
We are only sacrificing a part of eternity to turn the world around.

DR. GODOT
Who asked you?

A
It's the uninvited guest who does the good deed, and it's a good deed because the one who does it is disinterested.

B
Why don't you have your head examined. Surely you're dumber than you look.

DANIEL
Well. Shall we?
(Everyone nods yes, some grudgingly)
(BLACKOUT)

SCENE 3

Lights up. It is early afternoon near the Outer Hebrides. The apple tree has been replaced by a blue spruce. It is decorated for Christmas. Otherwise, the landscape is what it was in Scene 1.

    A
I was a working class baby.

    B
We all work.

    A
We just have different wardrobes.

    B
And some of us try to find out our family trees.

    DANIEL
You're welcome to yours. I prefer looking ahead to looking behind.

    A
Looking behind cannot guarantee good behavior.

    B
Or good taste.

    A
Or success in life.

    DANIEL
There are no guarantees.

    A
It does help if you try to find out what's the case and stick to it.

    DANIEL
That can be a pain.

B
Have you tried the opposite?
(General silence)

A
Aloha!

MISS LUST
Me again. I have the odd feeling I've been somewhere, but where, I do not know.

A
Me, too
(Everyone agrees)

MISS LUST
Well, memory is fallible, and probably just as well. If we remembered even the important things, we might save ourselves.

A
I like waiting.

MISS LUST
It certainly doesn't require much effort.

DANIEL
And you're waiting –

A
– for Godot.

B
I'm beginning to detect the familiar.

MISS LUST
Wait! My memory! It has come back! We were in heaven, and we have returned to earth –

           A
— to be useful.

           B
Lord.

        DANIEL
Alleluia.

           A
Pozzo!
(Who is entering)
And Lucky!
(Ditto)

           B
Shall we tell them?

        DANIEL
Is the truth serviceable?

           A
They'd never believe a word.

           B
They never did.

       MISS LUST
They are out of practice when it comes to the truth. In fact, they each have only half a personality, the dark half.

           A
I always thought they were amoral.

           B
Truth for them is an enigma.

           A
Wrapped in plastic

DANIEL
Covered in –

B
Manure.

A
Let us leave them thinking so – for the time being.

B
Now what?
(A whispers to B. They all leave, except for POZZO and LUCKY)

POZZO
(Muttering to himself)
Domination without vanity is getting awfully dull. You! Lucky! Stand!
(LUCKY complies)

POZZO
(Continued)
It's always the same thing. And we're the only two here. I can't even have a decent conversation, and I've been lying to myself for years. There is no comfort in that. What if I can no longer talk to myself? Talk about solitude! Stand! Lucky! Stand!
(LUCKY stands. He has been wilting while POZZO delivers his monologue)

POZZO
(Continued)
I seem to have fallen into a pit.
(LUCKY falls over. POZZO doesn't notice)

POZZO
(Continued)
My mind is dark – it always was – I have no heart – never did – I have sold my soul, not even to the highest bidder – I was being sly, to cover my desire – money is no good, I already own

everything – and I belong to no one. I can't even die. Not that I want to. Death does not attract me – only life – of a kind – I make life hell for Lucky – that is why I call him Lucky – it is a joke.

(He groans)

(LUCKY begins to make noises with his mouth which slowly bring POZZO to a blind rage)

POZZO
(Continued)

Beast! Turd! Beggar! Slave! Oh, my head, my head. I cannot bear to be alive. I am afraid of death. I bring death to life. The moon is in eclipse – Juno Queen of Heaven would not see me if she tried. Things are heating up. My life lies. I lie. I am half the world and I lie.

(He falls down and begins to have convulsions)

Lord, the devil is breaking my bones! This is agony!

(After a while, the fit subsides, and POZZO falls asleep)

(Meanwhile, LUCKY wakes up, takes off his ropes and quietly decamps)

(Enter A and B)

A
He seems to be sleeping.

B
He needs it.

A
Did you hear him howling?

B
Indeed.

A
Was it his soul?

B
I think his feet hurt.

A
Well, I was beginning to think he didn't have a soul.

B
Everyone has one who wants one.

A
Is he going to wake up?

B
Yes. After what to his sleeping soul seems like an eternity of pain.

A
Which is for us only thirty minutes.

B
That's a good trick.

A
One of our better ploys. It's called "a fold in time saves nine."

B
Do you dream?

A
All the time. It's my specialty.

B
Well, I approve of the results.

A
Thank you.

B
You said thirty minutes?

>A

Time is collapsible. Your patience is too. Ready?
(POZZO stands up, but is still asleep. He is sleep-walking)

>A

Pozzo!
(POZZO turns to A)

>A

Tell us what you love!

>POZZO

Nobody.

>A

And what do you possess?

>POZZO

Nothing.

>A

Who are you?

>POZZO

Nobody.

>A

What are you?

>POZZO

Nothing.

>A

How do you see?

>POZZO

I see nothing.

>A

Where do you feel?

POZZO
Nowhere.

B
Pozzo, is this what you want?
(POZZO says nothing)
(Pause)

B
(Continued)
Pozzo, do you want nothing?

POZZO
I want everything.
(Pause)

A
Everything is nothing
(BLACKOUT)

SCENE 4

Lights up. Tea time. GODOT is having tea with A and B.

GODOT
So you see, that is my dilemma. Pozzo was quite accurate – along with you, A. Everything is infinite – and everything is therefore nothing. Reality requires boundaries, just as sense – or language – requires rules. Without rules there is chaos and without boundaries there is nothing. My problem now is that the boundaries are breaking down. We must find a way to build them back up, or the universe is lost.

A
Milk or lemon?

GODOT
Milk, please, with two sugars.

B
What can we do?

GODOT
Quite simple. This all happened because I was dead – by choice. In the interim the universe was handed over to the forces of darkness – and remains there except for this earth.

A
We are the last refuge of the light?

GODOT
Yes, with a little bit of cleaning. You are very inconspicuous, and for the moment you remain overlooked. Soon enough that will not be the case. And I have taken the trouble to tell you so. You ought to be prepared to defend yourselves, and then the rest of creation as well.

B
That's a bit stiff.

A
Ready for Star Wars?

GODOT
The threat is already present.

A
What do you do with a threatening presence?

GODOT
First, you talk to them; then you take the threat out of their hands; then you talk some more.

A
It's called disarming the threatening presence?

GODOT
Yes.

B
It seems to work.

GODOT
Yes.

B
So far.

A
If we spend our time as peace-makers, how do we support ourselves?

B
The last carrot is gone.

A
No more rutabaga.

GODOT
You both are invited to earn a handsome salary as managers.

A
Managers are generally paid more for their services than the common man.

GODOT
That is because their responsibilities are greater. Their failures affect their colleagues, their superiors and their subordinates. If the common man fails, it is he alone who suffers.

B
And his family.

A
If he has one.

B
That is why some people avoid the upper crust: it is a risky place, and one is constantly in danger of being held up.

A
Or celebrated.

A
Same thing.

GODOT
I shall try to make your profile quite flat.

A
Thank you.

B
Well.
(LUCKY appears, well-dressed and nicely groomed)
(He putters about)

A
What about Pozzo and Lucky?

B
Those who rule the world must learn to rule themselves.

A
And we're their learning material?

GODOT
Yes.

B
Then we are making them a gift of ourselves.

A
But that is all we have.

GODOT
Yes.

B
You will find that they do not realize what they have.

GODOT
Until it is no longer theirs.

A
And then it is too late.

B
Yes.

A
At which point they are reduced to nothing.

GODOT
That is how things are arranged.
(BLACKOUT)

SCENE 5

(A and B enter)

>A

Life sometimes limps.

>B

Tell me.

>A

Let's go back to heaven! Things there were certain.

>B

Up to you.
(They remain fixed to the spot)

>A

Seems to me I've done this before.

>B

Out of different motives.
(They smile)
(MISS LUST enters)

>A

Miss Lust, how are you?

>MISS LUST

Travelin'. It's so fatiguin'.

>A

By train?

>MISS LUST

No. Foot.

>A

Any customers?

MISS LUST
We are ghosts.

A
I forgot. But now that we are here, everything is back to where it was. What is that on your nose?

MISS LUST
Oh, a bit of –

A
Take my handkerchief.
(MISS LUST breaks down)

MISS LUST
It is so difficult to be dead here. In heaven I was happy. Here I am constantly confronted with my past. It is so hard to see what you were, it reminds you of what you might have become. I would like to move on.

B
(To A)
She's in fine shape.

A
At least she knows where she fits in.

B
We may find her something to do here.

A
Something useful.

B
Besides sex.

A
She may need retraining.

B
That is all right. Miss Lust!

MISS LUST
Yes?

B
Come with us. We think we may cook up something for you to do: something fun.

MISS LUST
Really?
(They all exit)

SCENE 6

A
We must respect our feelings – they are guides to ourselves, and to others.

B
Some people do not relish their feelings.

A
Some people do not relish the feelings of others.

B
The subject is inexhaustible.

A
I don't think so.

B
I hope you're right.

A
I knew someone once who deliberately set himself up all the time.

B
Yes, and then he got knocked down. It was edifying.

A
And then he got back on his feet –

B
– and did it again.

A
It was Godot. In his youth.

B
Did we know him then?

A
I don't know.

B
Why did he do it?

A
He wanted to be human.
(B shakes his head)

A
Are we human?

B
I think we have graduated.

A
Thank goodness.

B
Of course, if you're alone, there's no one to knock you down.

A
Yes.

B
Are we alone?

A
You are here with me.

B
You are here with me.

A
I have always trusted you.

B
It's mutual.

    A
You have never failed me, even when sex was in question.

    B
Sex is not everything.

    A
Mr. Tops helped most graphically.

    B
I was not jealous.

    A
No, you were an angel. You understood my problem.

    B
You understood mine.

    A
I love you. I love you more than I deserve.

    B
Me, too.

    A
How long will all this last?

    B
I guess Godot has the answer to that: until we get tired of it.

    A
Then let's take our time.

    B
I shall follow you beyond imagination.

    A
Perhaps we should get married.

    B
That is beyond imagination.

A

It is nothing, when you are contemplating the end of time.

B

Well, let's stick it out here for a few more years and see how we feel then.

A

You were always cautious.

B

We have done quite well so far without ceremony. Why mess it all up?

A

You're a genius.

B

I try to be sensible.

A

Did you ever feel guilty about the sex act?

B

No. It was an expression of my love. Why should I feel guilty about love?

(Silence)

B

(Continued)

That is why I cannot enjoy one-night stands.

A

There is no love.

B

I require warm-ups, dinner parties, book-fairs, bicycling, even TV. I do not treat love lightly.

A

Love does not treat us lightly.

B
Just so.

A
Think of it. I have been loving you in so many ways for 2001 years, and I didn't know it.

B
I did.

A
I always get nervous when people start telling each other how much they love one another.

B
People talk a lot.

A
I never cared for gossip.

B
Me neither. It is tinsel.

A
Dressed in words.

B
It is often fatal.

A
It has destroyed many good people.

B
Godot was a good person.

A
I thought he was just acting.

B
If so, it was because acting was his life.

    A
Some acts are hard to comprehend.
    B
We must try to see clearly.
    A
We are not Gods.
    B
No. But we needn't all be fools.
    A
Do you know what comes next?
    B
More love?
    A
Heavens preserve us.
    B
Yes. Heaven. That's it.
    A
But we were there just a short time ago.
    B
Let's follow the Little Prince and go back.
    A
It's less trouble.
    B
I don't think we are really welcome here.
    A
No one talks to us.
    B
They don't let us know that they are thinking of us.

> A

Yes they do.

> B

You're right, I am wrong – they do show some care.

> A

Some people are very solicitous.

> B

I suppose we should stay and encourage the trend.

> A

It would help.

> B

I don't know anybody's name.

> A

It would help to ask: you would simply be showing your interest. It would be a compliment.

> B

Are we interested?

> A

Let us try it out for a few years.

> B

We are free to leave at any time.

> A

Yes. That is how things are arranged.

(BLACKOUT)

SCENE 7

TOFF 2
Well, Miss Lust, are you prepared to surprise us?

MISS LUST
Excuse me?

TOFF 2
We have all been invited to Mr. Puech's for a party.

MISS LUST
Who is Mr. Puech?

TOFF 2
You will see when you meet him.

MISS LUST
His picture makes him look a little crazed.

TOFF 2
He is a busy man.

MISS LUST
I am a busy woman.

TOFF 1
Try him on for size.

MISS LUST
I am not coming out of retirement for anyone, least of all Mr. Puech. What an ugly name.

TOFF 1
I will keep an eye out for you.

MISS LUST
Are you proposing a pecuniary emolument?

TOFF 1

Well…

MISS LUST

I would sooner be the Hermit on the Mount than sell myself. My self is all I have. Everyone seems to like money. It is like a disease, an infectious disease. I prefer not to go to extremes, even with money.

TOFF 1

It is best to be comfortable without extravagance.

TOFF 2

I am comfortable without anything.

TOFF 1

That helps.

TOFF 2

Not everyone born into the upper middle class ends up writing poetry for nothing.

MISS LUST

You need a sideline.

TOFF 2

You, my dear.

MISS LUST

What?

TOFF 2

We make a striking pair. If we get the right invitations, we can live off the fat of the land.

MISS LUST

You mean crumbs from above.

TOFF 2

Mr. Puech seems to be willing to give us some practice. In return, I shall dedicate my next poem to him. I think he will be pleased.

TOFF 1

Well, are you ready?

TOFF 2

Yes.

MISS LUST

I need to practice.

TOFF 2

Wing it, dear. They'll love you in any case.

MISS LUST

Oh!

TOFF 1

You can come as Glinda the Good.

TOFF 2

I shall be the Muse of Poetry.

TOFF 1

I shall be the Oracle of Delphi.

MISS LUST

I always wanted my future told.

TOFF 1

I shall try.

TOFF 2

You can practice on tea-leaves.

MISS LUST

Oh!

TOFF 2
If you need help, I'll be watching.

MISS LUST
Thank you.

TOFF 1
Remember: courage.

TOFF 2
I'll pick you up if you fall down.

MISS LUST
Ready.
(They all exit together)

SCENE 8

MISS LUST
But I do not want your money, Mr. Puech. I cannot sell myself into slavery.

MR. PUECH
We are all free to be slaves, Miss Lust. And I offer you the most attractive opportunity.

MISS LUST
Your money is worth nothing, Mr. Puech, and so are you.

MR. PUECH
(Momentarily silent, then produces a large wad of bills and says)
I have further reserves.
(MISS LUST turns her back on PUECH and goes as far away from him as she can)
(TOFF 1 and TOFF 2 enter)

TOFF 1
Ah. Perhaps we should withdraw.

TOFF 2
We always get our timing wrong.

TOFF 1
(Looking lovingly at TOFF 2)
Except once.

TOFF 2
Miss Lust! You're early.

MISS LUST
I needed some warm-up.

TOFF 1
Looks like you got it.

MISS LUST
He makes propositions. It is very tiresome. I suppose he has not found out.

TOFF 2
Found out what?

MISS LUST
We are ghosts.

TOFF 2
Miss Lust, as long as we are here, we are not ghosts.

MISS LUST
What about A and B? They van disappear at will.

TOFF I
They are a special case. They have earned a little cream on their cake.

MISS LUST
Then I shall need some money.
(She looks for PUECH)

TOFF 2
Only enough to live on, with something thrown in for lollipops.

MISS LUST
Thanks. Who's the sugar daddy?

TOFF 1
Daniel. He's been working his tail off for us all.
(MISS LUST melts)

MISS LUST
He always was a dear. I guess he could be a pupil. I owe it to him.

TOFF 2

Careful.

MISS LUST

Ok.

(Enter A and B)

A

A morgue.

B

Madame Tussaud's.

A

Parliament.

B

Wherever.

A

Are you being persnickety?

B

What?

A

Snap, snap, snap.

B

What?

A

Where is your hearing?

B

What?

A

I shall die.

B

Yes.

A
Oh, God.

B
Yes.

A
I give up.

B
So do I.

TOFF 1
A! B!

A & B
Halloo!

A
We have given up.

TOFF 1
Don't throw your chips away. We are all about to cash them in, with Mr. Puech here.

TOFF 2
Wealth is transient.

B
So is life, but I don't cash it in.

A
You can cash in anything.
(B pulls out a gnawed rutabaga from his pocket)
(Everyone looks at the rutabaga)

B
You must be right.

TOFF 2
Save it. You may need it.

                A

Good idea. Look; here come Fish and Miss Primp.
(PROF. FISH and MISS PRIMP enter)

                PROF. FISH

Delighted.
(He shakes hands all round)

                MISS PRIMP

Delighted.
(She shakes hands, etc.)

                A

Still fishing, Professor?

                PROF. FISH

For trout, yes. Metaphorically speaking, no. It is too much for a man my age. The trout bite, but my feet freeze.

                MISS PRIMP

You can always warm them, dear.

                PROF. FISH

Yes, we are engaged to be married.

                B

What a generous gesture.

                A

Do not make fun of hope, nor of gestures.

                B

Hope is not exactly a hot number.

                A

We have already established there are no guarantees. Do you wish to change our minds?

                B

No.

PROF. FISH
We are happy.

MISS PRIMP
Yes.

A
You have our sincere good wishes.

PROF. FISH
Thank you.

A
We need something to drink.

MISS PRIMP
Allow me.
(A WAITER goes by and she orders drinks)
(Re-enter WAITER followed by MISS LUST)

WAITER
(To MISS PRIMP)
Ma'am.

MISS PRIMP
Thank you.
(WAITER serves other drinks)

MISS LUST
(Eyeing WAITER)
If only I were back in business.

MR. PUECH
Ah! Miss Lust.
(PUECH places his hand on MISS LUST's derriere – and then finds he can't get it off)

MISS LUST
Mr. Puech! You are being naughty.
(PUECH's hand is still stuck to MISS LUST's bottom)

MISS LUST
(Continued)
Well!
(She moves away, dragging PUECH with her)
Are you deaf?

MR. PUECH
It is not my fault.

MISS LUST
It most certainly is. Ouch!

MR. PUECH
Ouch!

MISS LUST
You are too fresh! I should go back into business just to give you a lesson. Ouch!

MR. PUECH
Miss Lust…

MISS LUST
Creep!
(She starts swatting PUECH with her purse)

MR. PUECH
Ouch! Oh!

MISS LUST
I need a drink. Mr. Puech, don't try to buy me off. I know your type: you are a grab-snatcher. Well snatch someone else's grab – or grab someone else's snatch. I will not be violated by a drunken plutocrat. You are all the same. You think that because you have money, the world is yours. Well it isn't. One red rose, even with thorns, is worth ten Puechs, or a hundred. Ouch! Stop that! You should be committed. Oh! Ouch!

MR. PUECH
It's not my fault. I just meant..

MISS LUST
You didn't mean anything. You never do. Your life has no meaning. It begins and ends with dollar signs. The sun at dawn is my witness: you live a lie. You are a monomaniac, at the very least. And women, for you, are toys, pleasant but expendable. Well, I am not available, nor expendable. And you cannot have me, however attached you are. So take your filthy hand somewhere else. You may have earned money, but you have not earned me.

(She takes a swipe at PUECH and his hand comes free)
Ah!

MR. PUECH
(Weary)
That was hell.

MISS LUST
Some people's heaven can turn out that way.

B
(To PUECH)
Perhaps you should stick to finance.

MR. PUECH
This is my house, not yours. I'll not be laughed at.

A
Mr. Puech, ridicule is better than hypocrisy, don't you think? It clears the air and provides amusement at the same time. I know, you are not amused. I am sorry, but that is the only way to get through the serious little dramas of day-to-day existence: with a smile. There!

(PUECH smiles)

MR. PUECH
But this is my house. I own it. You are my guests.

A
You are backsliding, Mr. Puech. Try that smile again.
(PUECH tries and fails)

A
(Continued)
Well, some practice should help. Come with me.
(They retire to a corner of the room)

MISS LUST
That was too much.

B
Such devotion

TOFF 1
He was enthralled.

TOFF 2
You are a nice shape.

MISS LUST
Yes, but please don't touch.

TOFF 2
Ever think of marriage?

MISS LUST
It is rapidly becoming an attractive possibility.

TOFF 1
Where is Godot?

MISS LUST
Please. I am not that upwardly mobile.

TOFF 1
You will settle for…?

MISS LUST
None of your business. My plans are my own. So is my life.

B
Good.
(A and PUECH return to party)

A
Mr. Puech, it turns out, loves money more than Miss Lust. I have the evidence.

MISS LUST
We do not need evidence. We need trust.

MR. PUECH
I want my money.

B
There you are.
(An avalanche of dollar bills covers PUECH. His head appears after a few moments)

MR. PUECH
Oooohh.

B
That is what I like to see: a man immersed in his work.

MISS LUST
Mr. Puech, your task is to count every dollar. When you are through, you may keep it all. But, if you make a mistake, or lose your place, you must start over.

MR. PUECH
(Already counting)
3, 4, 5, 6, 7, 8, 9…

MISS LUST
Some party. I get raped and Puech gets the booby prize: and he doesn't know it.

   B
He will.
(A giggles)

   A
This is poetic justice.

   B
What's poetic about it?

   A
Ask the expert.
(He looks at TOFF 2)

   TOFF 2
It is poetic because it is simultaneously metaphorical and real. Mr. Puech is a metaphor. His money is real. Or perhaps it's the other way around. Same difference.

   A
But money is just paper.

   B
Tell him that.

   TOFF 2
He will find it out.

   A
If money is just paper, what use is it?

   B
It is very efficacious in the loo.

   A
Oh.
(B giggles)

   B
Let's blow this joint.
(Exit all but PUECH, who continues counting)

SCENE 9

PUECH is still counting his money. There are two piles of bills; on his left, the counted, on his right, the uncounted. He looks quite content and is humming to himself. MISS LUST enters.

    MISS LUST

Well, Puech, still counting?

(PUECH ignores this)

    MISS LUST

(Continued)

Fascinating, isn't it? Like solitaire. It could go on indefinitely.

(As an afterthought)

How old are you?

(PUECH is becoming annoyed)

    MISS LUST

(Continued)

You know, we have said this before: money can only buy what is for sale. Mr. Puech, you have sold yourself.

(PUECH loses a beat)

    MISS LUST

(Continued)

Ooops. You don't want to begin again. You are not young, and you have a lot of work ahead of you.

(Gesturing to the two piles, etc.)

I never cared for accountancy. Too many numbers. They get mixed up, and then you have problems. Of course, you can blame them on someone else. Look at Pozzo. Look at Lucky. Humanity is, I suppose, not to blame. You, Mr. Puech, are working alone. So all the responsibility is yours. Very courageous of you. I would not do it, even if I could count. But

I do not count, so I don't.
(PUECH loses his count)

MR. PUECH

Damnation woman! Why do you talk?

MISS LUST

All women talk, in between ironing shirts.

MR. PUECH

You have ruined my work. I was up to 1,782.

MISS LUST

Then go on to 1,783.

MR. PUECH

Oh. Thank you.

MISS LUST

I try to help.

MR. PUECH

But I know I lost a few, listening to you.

MISS LUST

You could begin again.

MR. PUECH

This is too much.

MISS LUST

Of course it is.
(PUECH looks very unhappy)

MISS LUST

(Continued)

You are used to having some one do it for you.
(PUECH looks disconsolate)

MISS LUST
(*Continued*)
Now you are stuck with the grind. But it has taught you something, hasn't it?

MR. PUECH
I hate it.

MISS LUST
What do you hate?

MR. PUECH
(*After a long pause*)
I hate money. It has destroyed my life.

MISS LUST
Look at A and B – they never had money, and they survived.

MR. PUECH
We seem to live at the extremes.

MISS LUST
Bravo. And –

MR. PUECH
I am lost.

MISS LUST
Only your money is lost, Mr. Puech. You are still here.
(*PUECH looks around, brightens*)

MR. PUECH
You mean I don't need this money?

MISS LUST
Of course not. There are many other ways to live, most of them healthy. Take your pick. You will have enough to live on.

MR. PUECH
I like roses.

MISS LUST
So do I. What is your favorite color?

MR. PUECH
Red – but I really like almost all colors equally.

MISS LUST
Red. That is the color of love.
(PUECH tunes in)

MISS LUST
(Continued)
Yes. You are right on target, Mr. Puech, with red roses.

MR. PUECH
What do you want me to do?

MISS LUST
What do you want to do, Mr. Puech? That is the question.

MR. PUECH
My house has a garden. And there are many roses. And some of them are red.

MISS LUST
You are a genius, Mr. Puech. Do you know what a garden is for?

MR. PUECH
To live in.

MISS LUST
Hoorah!
(PUECH begins to cry)
(MISS LUST joins in)

MISS LUST
Our world is a garden. It was once beautiful.

MR. PUECH
It will be beautiful again.

MISS LUST
(Wiping away a few tears)
Truth always moves me, Mr. Puech. You too, I see. Well, what about the roses?

MR. PUECH
To work!

MISS LUST
To work!

MR. PUECH
To the gift of our garden.

MISS LUST
Let us move forward –

MR. PUECH
– And undo the past.

MISS LUST
Let us explore the unexplored.

MR. PUECH
And be happy at home.

MISS LUST
Mr. Puech, you are a wonder.

MR. PUECH
Miss Lust, the world is a wonder, and we are in it.
(They join hands, do a little dance, and then exit toward the garden)
(BLACKOUT)

SCENE 10

    A
What are we doing?

    B
Are we doing something? In the dark?

    A
I am breathing.

    B
You could stop.

    A
It doesn't work. I tried.

    B
Ah, life.

    A
Is there a light?
(Lights up. They are in PUECH's garden)

    B
I thought I smelled something.

    A
Oooh. Roses.

    B
It is a jungle.

    A
We could help prune.

    B
I thought Puech was counting dollars.

A
Me, too.

B
He has become a gardener.

A
In the closet.

B
Nonsense. Being a gardener is no reason for shame.

A
Are we ashamed?

B
Are we alive?

A
This garden needs help.

B
Where is Puech?

(PUECH's head appears from a mass of blooms)

MR. PUECH
Ah, visitors! We are not ready for visitors, but you are welcome, anyway.

A
Thank you.

(B nods)

A
(Continued)
Do you need help?

MR. PUECH
Well, not really. It will take time. It may take a lifetime. But I am patient.

      A
You are also determined.

      B
This must be a new world for you, Mr. Puech.
(PUECH smiles)

      A
Do you think we could re-anoint you? Why not pronounce your name peach?
(PEACH beams)

      A
Good.

      B
Well, Mr. Peach, welcome to the world. It has been our garden for 2001 years, more or less. We went where we could –

      A
And ended up on a stony promontory near the Outer Hebrides.

      B
We were safe from the world.

      A
The world was safe from us.

      B
There were no roses. But we had visitors, even near the Outer Hebrides.

      A
And now we have a garden to visit: with roses.

      B
It is too much.

A
And you, Mr. Peach. I can see you have made several correct choices.
(PEACH blushes)

A
(Continued)
And you are just beginning to appreciate the results.
(PEACH nods)

MR. PEACH
There will be time –

A
To prepare a face –

B
To meet the faces that you meet…

A
You are on the right road, Mr. Peach.

B
Don't let the tricky parts throw you, Mr. Peach.

MR. PEACH
They already have.

A
Then you are prepared.

MR. PEACH
You got it.

A
Mr. Peach, you are on the right road. We must all, sooner or later, go to school.

B
And school is not a building.

MR. PEACH
It is a state of mind.

A
Oooh, I love it,

MR. PEACH
It is a capacity.

A
Is comedy allowed?

MR. PEACH
Without question. It was comedy that moved me.
(A and B smile broadly)

B
You may have felt uncomfortable –

A
(With a smile)
You survived.
(BLACKOUT)

SCENE 11

GODOT is alone onstage as the lights go up. GODOT swats at fly.

GODOT
This place ought to be debugged.
(Enter POZZO, tied to a chain. LUCKY follows, directing POZZO)

LUCKY
Right, left. Left. Right. Stop!

POZZO
Bugs? It is just Mother Nature. Birds live on bugs.

LUCKY
Barn swallows.

GODOT
What?

POZZO
Barn swallows live on bugs. If you carry things far enough in the food chain, we live on barn swallows.

GODOT
Oh.
(Pause)
How are the politicians?

POZZO
We are thriving.

GODOT
You have changed roles.

POZZO
Hardly.

LUCKY
He lost the election.

GODOT
But there are only two of you.

LUCKY
His ballot was invalidated. Non compos mentis.

GODOT
Oh. Who figured that one out?

POZZO
I did.

GODOT
This is a vicious circle.

POZZO
It is a circle, but it is not vicious.

LUCKY
He is allowed to wash dishes.
(POZZO beams)

LUCKY
(Continued)
Everyone is happy.
(Looks around)

GODOT
I am glad to hear it.
(Looks around doubtfully)
(Pause)
Do you have company?
(LUCKY tries to speak, but POZZO gets there first)

POZZO
We are each other's own best company.

LUCKY
If we get tired of one arrangement, its opposite is always possible.

POZZO
That is when we have an election.

GODOT
Oh.

POZZO
I am liberal.

LUCKY
I am conservative.

POZZO
When we get tired of that –

GODOT
You switch.

LUCKY
Yes.

GODOT
What does liberal mean?

POZZO
Whatever you want. They'll make room for you.

GODOT
And the same for conservative?

LUCKY
Just about. The liberals say the conservatives care only about themselves.

GODOT
Do they have friends?

LUCKY
Yes.

GODOT
Do they have family?

LUCKY
Yes.

GODOT
Do they have charities?

LUCKY
Yes.

GODOT
Then I cannot see that the liberals are fair with the conservatives.

LUCKY
Some conservatives are wealthy.

GODOT
I suppose some liberals are, too.

LUCKY
But they don't get picked on.

GODOT
It sounds as though the liberals are exploiting the opportunity to make their opponents feel guilty.

LUCKY
Bingo.

GODOT
Do liberals ever feel guilty?

LUCKY
All the time. It is the fault of the conservatives.

GODOT
It seems you all want to be happy, but you don't know how.

LUCKY
So.

GODOT
Why not choose new goals?

LUCKY
What?

POZZO
What?

GODOT
Well, why not be in favor of someone other than yourselves?

LUCKY
I am against abortion.

POZZO
Conservative.

LUCKY
I am in favor of free trade.

POZZO
Middle-of-the-road.

LUCKY
Hooray for the Sandanistas!

POZZO
Very liberal.

LUCKY
I –

GODOT
Enough.

POZZO
You see? One label won't do. We need several, and the chance to change over time.

LUCKY
But that is more work.

GODOT
It may provide better answers.
(General silence)

GODOT
(Continued)
By the way, I would leave room for the individual.

LUCKY
I would, too. I think we've been railroaded.

POZZO
Surprise, surprise.

LUCKY
We did it to ourselves.

POZZO
Surprise, surprise. We are not very good politicians.

LUCKY
We can think.
(Pause)
What do we do now?

GODOT
Lie low.

(LUCKY drops his rope. Chains fall from POZZO, who doesn't notice – he is lost in his lucubrations and strikes a grand pose, totally unawares. LUCKY takes his cue from POZZO. For the first time in their history, they appear human, stately but vulnerable. Soon enough, they will trust each other. From that, everyone will take his cue)
(SLOW FADE)

SCENE 12

A
It is very odd.

B
What?

A
Odd. It's peculiar.

B
What is peculiar?

A
That we are still here.

B
Yes. We are the eyes of Paradise. We are beginning to be responsible.

A
You tell that to the people and you'll get royally walloped.

B
Am I talking?

A
Only to me.

B
So. Are you talking?

A
Only to you.

B
What about the obliquity of time?

A
I think we should leave time to the philosophers.

B
You can count on it, they will confuse the issue.

A
They will confuse themselves.

B
That is philosophy.

A
Ouch.

B
Your hair is full of burrs. Where have you been sleeping?

A
By your tent.

B
Oh. I thought we generally shared in our sleeping arrangements.

A
I like to be alone sometimes.

B
Oh.

A
It allows my heart to breathe.

B
Mine, too.

A
Thank you.
(B smiles and pecks A's cheek)

           A
(Continued)
　I am melting again.

           B
　Save it! For tonight – in both tents; we can alternate, if you like.

           A
　I've got my eye on you, not the tents.
(B smiles again and adds a peck to the first one)

           A
　I don't think we look our age.
(Eyeing a small mirror he has pulled out of his pocket)

           B
　We look older.

           A
　Nonsense. I would say you look 40 and I look 39.

           B
　What's the difference?

           A
　You're supposed to know more than me.
(B beams but says nothing)

           A
(Continued)
　Life is not always generous.

           B
　At least we have not shriveled up into grasshoppers.

           A
　No. We are well preserved.

           B
　For what purpose?

A
We are witnesses.

B
You mean we see everything and report it upstairs?

A
Yes.

B
I hope we stay here permanently.

A
London would overwhelm us in two seconds.

B
I cannot overhear more than three conversations at a time.

A
London would be impossible. Peach's party was enough.

B
Me, too.

A
Here we entertain one guest at a time.

B
If they come.

A
Yes.

B
It teaches tolerance.

A
And forgiveness.

B
Where appropriate.

A
Where there is crime –

B
There is punishment.

A
In the end we all dig our own graves.

B
It is called life.
(They are silent for a while)

A
We do not spill the milk.

B
We spill the truth.

A
It is not a happy job sometimes.

B
A mess is a mess.

A
What did that man Goethe say?

B
If everyone swept his own threshold, the world would be clean.

A
It is, here.
(They smile at one another)

B
I wish we could help further.

A
We do.

                B
Nobody says thank you.

                A
Nobody says a thing.

                B
(Shouting)
Where is everybody?
(There is an echo, then silence)
If they told me this was earth, I wouldn't believe it.

                A
Why not?

                B
Look.
(They do so)

                A
Perhaps we're in Hell.

                B
It's a possibility.

                A
Why stay?

                B
Ineptitude on the part of the Authorities.

                A
They probably forgot we were here. It's like the Army.

                B
Are we supposed to be fighting someone?

                A
Ourselves.

B
Why?

A
We are expected to change our feelings?

B
No thank you.

A
We're off to a wonderful start.

B
What I have always done is all that I can think of doing.

A
Courage, yes. Imagination, no.

B
I give up.

A
Nonsense. You are on the threshold of a miracle and you crap out. Collect yourself. We're going for a ride.

(A two person bicycle appears. They get on and ride off)
(LIGHTS DIM)

SCENE 13

The Stage is bare except for a table with a telephone. The telephone begins to ring. No one appears. The telephone rings again. No one appears again. The telephone stops ringing. A and B rush in just in time to greet the silence.

    A
All that riding.

    B
Are you sure it was ringing?

    A
No. But it might have been.

    B
We will never know.

    A
It could have been Godot.

    B
With instructions.

    A
Where to meet.

    B
What to do.

    A
We already know what to do.

    B
Yes. We don't need Godot to tell us that.

        A
Our first meeting was helpful.
(Pause)

        B
Where is everybody?

        A
On a picnic.

        B
Oh.

        A
What if it was Godot? We might have missed something important.

        B
He'll call again

        A
If it was him.
(Silence)

        A
(Continued)
    We missed the picnic too?

        B
Yes, Pozzo and Lucky made the arrangements. Here they come.
(POZZO and LUCKY arrive in business suits. They look very smart)

        B
(Continued)
(Sotto voce)
    This is too much.

            A
Shhh!

            B
(To POZZO)
A little respite, eh?
(POZZO nods and starts picking HIS teeth)

            B
(Continued)
Fine weather.
(POZZO belches)

            A
Good food, Mr. Pozzo?

          POZZO
Splendid.
(Pulls out menu)

          POZZO
(Continued)
(To A)
Here.

            A
Ohh! Cream of celery soup, quail, sherbet, Beef Wellington, salad, crepes flambees, cognac, cigars.

            B
With all that to tuck into, we could survive for another 2000 years.

            A
No problem.

            B
How was it, Mr. Pozzo?
(POZZO belches again)

B
(Continued)
   That good?

A
   Mr. Pozzo, you must try to include us all next time.
(POZZO resumes picking his teeth)

A
(Continued)
   Oral hygiene is very important.

B
   But not when you don't eat. There's nothing to pick.

A
   We have done very well at not eating.

B
   We have enough practice.

A
   We must have been dead.

B
   Mr. Pozzo, does Lucky participate in your gustatory extravaganzas?
(POZZO kicks LUCKY, who has fallen asleep on the floor)

A
   Back to square one.

B
   How long did that take?

A
   Two weeks.

B
   All that hard work. All those words.

A
It kept us busy.

B
Pozzo was busy.

A
Running this place is not easy, especially when it is depopulated.

B
All the rewards are empty.

A
That's appropriate.

B
Lucky is a slave by choice.

A
We are all free to be slaves.

B
I think I've heard that already.

A
It's still true.

(POZZO and LUCKY go off. MISS LUST appears)

MISS LUST
Oh, our man of the moment is not much to gauge goodness by.

B
That is not the business of rulers. If they are young they are foolish and want everything arranged to their own taste. When they are old, they are beyond redemption, and what they do is unmentionable.

A
I can mention it.

B
Please.

A
(Finger to lips)
Shhh.

B
Sometimes madness is inscrutable.

A
Perhaps we should be cynical for a while.

B
I'd rather be a hypocrite. It is less trouble.

A
It's a matter of judgement and discipline. Very few people advertise what they are for all the world to know.

B
Look at Godot.
(They both throw up their arms)
(BLACKOUT)

SCENE 14

A bathroom.

          MISS PRIMP
My bathtub is full of jello!

          LUCKY
"There's always room for jello."

          MISS PRIMP
In me, or in my bathtub?

          POZZO
Maybe I can buy my way out of this dessert.

          MISS PRIMP
(Handing POZZO a spoon)
Eat!
(They all begin to eat jello)
(BLACKOUT)

SCENE 15

A
Where is Miss Primp?

B
On a picnic. She's taking care of dessert.

A
Ooh. I love cheesecake.

B
I hear her specialty is jello. It is easy to prepare, especially in quantity.

A
She must be preparing for a trip to India.

B
What is this with India?

A
They are a former colony of the British, and inherited Socialism as their creed.

B
Socialism – Smocialism, as long as they learn to govern.

A
They follow the usual rules.

B
I wasn't aware there were rules.

A
It depends what game you want to play.
(Pause)
There are rules.

B
What happens if they are broken?

A
Heads roll.

B
Mine has always felt a bit loose.

A
It depends how you wear it.

B
Mine is always a bit peaked.

A
It is not your hair.

B
I shall talk to Miss Primp.
(He goes off)

A
Ahh. A moment of solitude. After almost 2,000 years. This is unexpected. Ahh.
(A lies down and dozes off. PEACH enters and begins gardening. A wakes up and screams)

A
(Continued)
Oh! Mr. Puech.

MR. PEACH
It is Peach, now, thank you. I have been baptized for the second time.

A
Like a boat, revamped and retitled.

MR. PEACH
No. With water, like a baby.

A
You have earned it.
(PEACH is silent)
(B re-enters)

B
Deserved what?

A
Religion

MR. PEACH
I was re-christened.

B
You needed a bath. That is all.

A
Religion is a kind of cold bath.

B
I like mine warm.

A
Hot or cold, it is all religion.

B
I have given it up.

A
There is so much to choose from: Hinduism, Buddhism, Islam, and many varieties of Christianity.

B
They can't all be true. It would not be logically possible.

A
Many things that are not logically possible happen anyway.

B
Just as well. It is the impossibilities that count.

A
I always inclined toward Heracleitus and the Tao.

B
The Tao?

A
Yes. It is Chinese. It multiplies its meanings as you go along.

B
It is like poetry.

A
Yes.

B
Where is Toff 2?

A
Who knows? You do not need an expert to read poetry. You need a sensibility.

B
What good is that?

A
It teaches us who we are.

B
Now I know why no one reads poetry.

A
What do we do with Peach here?

B
Let him dig. A rose is a rose, however many you plant. I can never tire of roses.

A
But he is planting only red roses.

B
Perhaps he is trying to tell us something.

A
Red is the color of love.

B
Mr. Peach?

MR. PEACH
At your service.

B
Are you in love?

MR. PEACH
I am firmly attached to red roses. It is the result of a misunderstanding.

B
Excuse me?

MR. PEACH
I had one rose with three thorns. By accident, I stepped on my rose at night, in the dark. And it died. I lost the one thing I cherished above all the universe. And then I came here and – surprise – found not one red rose, but hundreds, thousands even. Mother Nature is very generous here.

(Enter MISS LUST, LUCKY and POZZO)

MISS LUST
I see roses everywhere.

LUCKY
They are blinding in the light.

MISS LUST
It is Mr. Peach. He is planting roses, red roses, everywhere.

LUCKY
Even in the North Country.

MISS LUST
Some roses are very hardy.

POZZO
Yes!

LUCKY
Their perfume is heavenly.

B
Appropriate.

POZZO
Should we lend a hand?

MISS LUST
No...Let Mr. Peach do the roses. We could try fruit trees. Apples, plums, pears. Whatever will flourish in the appropriate place.
(DANIEL enters)

DANIEL
(To MISS LUST)
Miss Lust? May I help? Otherwise I shall go mad with boredom.

MISS LUST
I understand. Many of my clients turned to sex for the same reason: boredom. They had nothing better to do than indulge their fantasies, which they quickly wore out. Then came the real problems.
Yes, you may help me with my orchard. It will give your daily schedule some backbone. Everyone should have a garden – or an orchard.

DANIEL
At last! Someone who understands!

MISS LUST
But your fathers. They both understand, now. They have seen as much as anyone under the sun, except Godot. And he is not exactly under the sun.

DANIEL
Oh, Miss Lust…
(He bursts into tears)

MISS LUST
It is all right. You are young. If you are lucky, you will grow old.

B
Let us not be premature.

MISS LUST
(Ignoring B)
There! Now, crying helps. It always does. There…
(DANIEL blows his nose)

MISS LUST
Yes, you are honest with your feelings, and you are honest with yourself. That is good.

DANIEL
Miss Lust, may I marry you?

MISS LUST
What a nice proposal! But if I accepted, everyone else would object. Let us therefore marry. We can work as a team. In fact, most people do try to work as a team, at one point or another. We shall be extending ourselves to them. I do not think Godot would object. After all, he and I were once united, in fact even more than once. Yes, Daniel, I am prepared.
(She pulls out a ring, two rings, and hands one to DANIEL)

Watch out, Mr. Peach is the jealous type.

MR. PEACH

Nonsense. I am through with lust as well as money. I have had enough of snares. Once there was only one red rose in my life. Now, there are many.

MISS LUST

Mr. Peach, you are a marvel.

(MR. PEACH blushes and nods)

MISS LUST

(Continued)

Mr. Peach, we all love you.

(All the characters in the play appear onstage, except GODOT)
(They sing Happy Birthday)

MR. PEACH

But it is not my birthday.

MISS LUST

Every day is a birthday for one of your red roses.

(They all smile)
(Enter GODOT from above, on a swing)

GODOT

Mr. Peach, you are now married to the Goddess of Love, metaphorically speaking. You could not have chosen more fruitfully, or more wisely. Generosity is your creed, love your object, and a red rose is your method. Mr. Peach, you may have whatever in life you may wish.

MR. PEACH

One wish?

GODOT

Yes.

MISS LUST
I would wish for my old job back.

DANIEL
I would like my youth over again.

B
You are hardly grown up!

A
Shhh!

B
Well, I would wish to be rid of my headaches,

MR. PEACH
I wish that everyone, everywhere have a happy life.
(General astonishment)

B
What about you?

MR. PEACH
I have told you what I wish. And that is what will make me happy.

B
You're a marvel.

GODOT
I was not expecting such generosity, Mr. Peach. I am, well, I am surprised. After all, it is I who take the blame for catastrophes, death, disease, and dismemberment. No one has ever wished me well without ulterior motive, even when times were good and omens favorable. In fact, that is when people tend to forget me.

MR. PEACH
They couldn't say, "Thank you," could they?

GODOT
Yes.

MR. PEACH
Well, I am saying "thank you" for all of us. If you give me my wish, you should have in return what we all believe to be the most wonderful gift of all – love. You have given us life. We are trying to return the favor. No one should be without love, even you. Be kind to us, Mr. Godot. Accept our wish. It is universal.

GODOT
(Tears in eyes)
I shall. I cannot – I do not know what to say.

MISS LUST
Mr. Godot, try "thank you".

GODOT
(To all)
Thank you, thank you all. I suppose I have been preoccupied with everyone's affairs but my own. If I am to live amongst you, then I must indeed love.

MISS LUST
Righto. And we are all here to help. Even Mr. Tops is available.

GODOT
Bring him in!
(All smile)

TOPS
Mr. Godot, you are reputed to be a fast learner.

GODOT
Miss Lust was fast. I just tried to keep up.

TOPS
Please come with me.

(They exit for about two minutes, then reappear)

MISS LUST
Mr. Godot, I hope you take more time when the opportunity presents itself.

TOPS
Oh, he just used the techniques you taught him, with a few minor changes of emphasis. He is ready.

(MISS LUST nods and a splendid YOUNG MAN appears. Lights dim with spots on MISS LUST, MR. TOPS, GODOT and YOUNG MAN)

(Spot on GODOT, then BLACKOUT)

SCENE 16

GODOT
Dessert is such an anti-climax.

YOUNG MAN
You mean climax. We are not physicists. Physicists talk of anti-matter. It is our role in life to discuss what really matters, and it is not anti-matter, or anti-climax.

GODOT
Don't tell me after all I've been through that I'm stuck with a beauty who has a brain.

YOUNG MAN
You said it, not me.

GODOT
Would you care for some psychological testing?

YOUNG MAN
You have been quite adequate. I hope you give me a good report card.

GODOT
I do, I do. Only the clinical psychologists –

YOUNG MAN
Flush them down the drain. Their PhD's will not help them when they first encounter life. And you do not need a PhD to judge me. It is most likely a hindrance. I have never known your judgement to be wrong.

GODOT
I am disarmed!

(They laugh together)

GODOT
(Continued)
We are as well matched as A and B.

YOUNG MAN
Do you think we'll last 2,000 years?

GODOT
I never made predictions, and my expectations are always disappointed.

YOUNG MAN
So are mine. Let us therefore live for the present.

GODOT
Indeed.
(They kiss)

YOUNG MAN
We are scandalous.

GODOT
We need an audience. True love is invariably a scandal.

YOUNG MAN
I thought you were sexually ambiguous.

GODOT
Whatever suits at the time. I try not to force myself into each passing uniform.

YOUNG MAN
Let's try one on.
(They remove themselves upstage)
(A and B enter)

A
What a yucky atmosphere. I am sure there are voyeurs present.
(They look around)

B
Look! A couple, copulating!

A
We are not going to watch.

B
It might be educational.

A
Hey!

B
Ok, ok. I guess it's just as well not to try everything. We might learn more than is good for us.

A
Right.

B
Is there an echo here?

A
Right.

B
Cut it out.

A
Right.

B
I'm sorry, but I was intrigued by that couple.

A
It might derail our relationship. We spent 18 years with Mr. Tops – and lost Daniel. It seems foolish to throw all that wonderful experience out the window.

B
Now I know why we are still together: you have good sense.

A
You do, too. Only you like to indulge yourself.
(GODOT and YOUTH return)

GODOT
We have visitors!

YOUNG MAN
I am the youth.

A
Enchanted.

B
The same. I hope you did not notice us.

YOUNG MAN
It is all right. There is a little of the exhibitionist in all of us. I hope we were not dull.

B
Well, we didn't really look. A was not in favor of it. And I came around to his point of view.

YOUNG MAN
Then we can be real friends, not just porno stars.

A
Of course. That is what we were hoping.

GODOT
I have never been a star of any kind.

YOUNG MAN
Now don't get glorious.

GODOT
I'm not allowed to twinkle?

B
Is that what you call it?

                A
If you want to twinkle, do it for a psychologist, not us.
(Enter PROF. FISH)
                PROF. FISH
I am a clinical psychologist.
                B
Where did you find the time for that?
                PROF. FISH
While fishing.
                GODOT
I shall keep you in mind.
                PROF. FISH
At your service.
(He exits)
                B
If you need a money manager –
                GODOT
Me?????
                B
Oops.
                A
Oops.
                YOUNG MAN
A lawyer might prove useful. I hear a lot of libelous nonsense about you.
                GODOT
(To A and B)
I thought we had covered the topic of religion.

         B
It's an occupational hazard.

         GODOT
I can live with it.

         YOUNG MAN
Wait till they find out about me!

         GODOT
What am I supposed to do? Spend all my time talking to heads of stage, witty aristocrats and people of accomplishment? I know I would wear out my welcome very quickly. People like that are not usually fond of criticism, and I am not fond of lies. I prefer to leave them alone. It may teach them something.
(He looks around at everyone)
Meanwhile, we all have each other, as well as the prospect of further acquaintance.

         A
That is enough.

         B
Yup.

         YOUNG MAN
You're all wonders.

         GODOT
So are you. I hope it will last.

         YOUNG MAN
You are the guide – to eternity.

         GODOT
Let's not be extravagant.

         YOUNG MAN
Right. Well, let us follow the present forward, and we shall see what we shall see.

           GODOT
Agreed.
             A
Agreed.
             B
Agreed.
(LIGHTS DIM)

SCENE 17

GODOT
Are you digging a grave?

B
This is the resting place of our desires.

A
Our hopes.

B
For mankind.

GODOT
Don't humans have their own hopes?

A
You mean we're not responsible for everybody?

B
Each individual can figure out his desires for himself?

GODOT
It would help.

B
Everyone wants to make those he knows as like himself as possible.

GODOT
Look at what the religious have done.

B
Where is Yorick's skull?

A
Near the Outer Hebrides?

B
We must move to Denmark.

A
Why don't we save that for our next holiday.
(B looks discouraged)
(Enter POTENTATE, disguised as Hamlet)

A
Who are you?

POTENTATE
A potentate, disguised as Hamlet.

A
You are giving yourself away!

POTENTATE
Only my disguise, not my self. That is what a disguise is for. You give it away, and it comes right back as the latest fashion. I am always on show.

B
You get used to it.
(They look at the audience)

POTENTATE
I was not born yesterday.

B
Evidently.

A
What's next?

POTENTATE
Potentates are meant to wield power, but I find the results more satisfactory if I share power with my subjects; so, I have assumed, in my eminence, only a consultative role. Action I leave to actors.

A
So we see.

POTENTATE
What is your problem?

A
B and I have solved that one already. Mr. Tops gave us some pointers. But our son is a royal pain in the butt. And we are afraid he will never find a sensible style of life.

POTENTATE
What is his diet?

A
I don't know.

POTENTATE
You see! What we eat is what we are.

B
What you read is what you are.

POTENTATE
(Ignoring B)
If he is not eating properly, he can be open to all sorts of ill-humor. Does he exercise?

B
Only his tongue.

POTENTATE
You see! Our bodies can sabotage the brain, especially if the brain gets no rest.

B
Oh.

POTENTATE
You two could probably use a few laps around Hyde Park.

B
Ohh.

A
Ohh.

POTENTATE
Well, let us see to your son first...
(Exit A, B, and POTENTATE)

GODOT
Some potentate.
(TOFF 2 enters)

TOFF 2
I saw someone going off in the regalia of an Ottoman Emperor.

GODOT
It's Hamlet. He's preparing for a costume ball.

TOFF 2
I once went to one. It turned into an orgy.

GODOT
What did you do?

TOFF 2
I left. It was a health hazard.
(Pause)

TOFF 2
(Continued)
I did like the costumes. I went as one of Wellington's aides-decamp. It was a treat.

GODOT
I would not have been allowed to take sides. Perhaps I could have participated as an experienced intermediary. I've always wanted to dress up. In the few places I go these days, it is necessary to dress down.

TOFF 2
I shall see what I can find in the way of fancy military dress.

GODOT
Thank you.
(TOFF 2 exits)
(TOFF 2 then re-enters with a costume)

GODOT
Oh! This is splendid.

TOFF 2
Try it on.
(GODOT does so)

GODOT
Oh – I feel enthralling.

TOFF 2
The women will love you.

GODOT
They already do,

TOFF 2
Then they will love you some more.

GODOT
Don't tease.

TOFF 2
I'm serious.

GODOT
This is fun.

TOFF 2
You see.

GODOT
Yes.

TOFF 2
What a lesson.

GODOT
Yes.

TOFF 2
Where is the Potentate?
(Voice offstage)

POTENTATE
Coming!
(Enter POTENTATE with DANIEL)

DANIEL
I must have hurt them very early on.

POTENTATE
It is B that is hurt – and still is.

DANIEL
What can I do?

POTENTATE
Do you love him?

DANIEL
I love them both.

POTENTATE
So please be demonstrative. Cut the crap and treat them as they deserve. You are their future. They can help you survive.

DANIEL
You are too much.
(He starts crying)

POTENTATE
(Holding DANIEL)
You have a big heart.

DANIEL
So do A and B.
(He cries some more)

POTENTATE
Well. Let's not spend the day prone. Up and at 'em.
(They both get up)

TOFF 2
(To GODOT, who nods)
Ready? Everyone in costume. Present yourselves.
(A and B enter tgether dressed as harlequins)
(DANIEL appears as Howdy Doody)

B
(To A, pointing to DANIEL)
It's him. Don't say anything and he won't find out who we are.

A
B!

B
Watch.
(He walks up to Howdy Doody and, disguising his voice, speaks)

B
I am the Ace of Spades.

DANIEL
Nonsense.
(He laughs)
You are B. And there is A.

B
(His balloon punctured)
How did you know?

DANIEL
Body language. Mr. Tops taught me.

B
But you never studied with Mr. Tops.

DANIEL
I studied with you, incognito.

A
It is called being a child.

B
It is called being a faithful son.
(He embraces DANIEL)

POTENTATE
Let everyone keep the faith!
(At this point, the whole cast emerge onstage dressed for a ball. And that is what they have)

A
Ooohh. Well done.
(Lights up to watch the dancing and singing. SLOW FADE)

-*FINIS*-

Godot Imagine Godot
ಸಾ

A Comedy

INMATES

GODOT

DANIEL: Son of A and B

A: Visiting from the Outer Hebrides

MR. MALAPROP: B in disguise

UNCLE STURTEVANT: A Southerner suffering from
    megalomania

LADY DALY: A large black woman in her early thirties,
    manic-depressive with aggressive tendencies

DOTTIE DUMPLING: A maid, thin

LUCILLE OUTBACK: A Society Person

ALICE, PRINCESS OF LIVERMORE: An Oxford
    undergraduate

DR. LANCELOT HABIT: Resident-in-Chief

ACT I

SCENE 1

The action (or inaction) takes place at the Budinger Foundation, a psychiatric hospital located in Westchester Country about 30 minutes north of New York City. The set, which presents us with a single large interior, suggests a building of grand outer dimensions in the Georgian style, something like a Harvard House. The room we see is used alternately as a dining room, sitting room and for patient-doctor sondultations, as well as for meetings of the entire staff and patient population. It is clean, well-lit, and well-furnished, though not in any way luxurious.

>DANIEL
>My fathers are invisible.
>
>GODOT
>I have met them.
>
>DANIEL
>What did you think?
>
>GODOT
>Faithful and true. You know the tune?
>*(Singing)*
>"FAITHFUL AND TRUE..."

DANIEL
Must be disco. That was before my time.

GODOT
Time, time, I stretch myself thin sometimes. And there is Monsieur Malaprop. Come. Sit.

MR. MALAPROP
I like to stand. It is the only exercise you get around here.

GODOT
Up and down, up and down. Such is life.

DANIEL
Mr. Godot?

GODOT
Yes?

DANIEL
When are you leaving?

GODOT
I do not know. Or at least, I haven't been told. In my case, there are more than a few formalities that have to be settled.

MR. MALAPROP
Me, too.

GODOT
They are still trying to find out whether I am alive, and if so, who I am. For them, the name Godot has no reference. The philosophers would say it is an arrow with no target.

DANIEL
I hope to leave today.

MR. MALAPROP
So we all do.

DANIEL
I am planning to go back to my family.

GODOT
I have no family.

MR. MALAPROP
Of course you do. You are Godot.

GODOT
Ah, well. I guess that explains why I'm here.

DANIEL
Your family?

GODOT
Yes.

DANIEL
Oh. Don't they love you?

GODOT
They say they love me.

UNCLE STURTEVANT
(Looking up)
That's what my family says, too.

DANIEL
But you don't have a family.

UNCLE STURTEVANT
The brotherhood of souls is my family.

GODOT
You are lucky.

UNCLE STURTEVANT
I don't see why. After all, I am here with you, and you are all crazy.

MR MALAPROP
The pudding is in the proof.

LUCILLE OUTBACK
I am eighty-proof.

UNCLE STURTEVANT
How else could you stand all those cocktail parties?

LUCILLE OUTBACK
I know, what with the drinks and hors d'oeuvres, and collecting names.

DANIEL
Collecting names?

LUCILLE OUTBACK
Yes. I network - for a living. Names are a salable commodity.

DANIEL
Who do you sell them to?

LUCILLE OUTBACK
The highest bidder.

DANIEL
Is that what brought you here?

LUCILLE OUTBACK
I am here on business. There was one name I hadn't got.

DANIEL
Which one?

(LUCILLE OUTBACK points to GODOT)

DANIEL
Oh. His name is Godot. Everybody has his name already.

UNCLE STURTEVANT
And what good does it do them?

GODOT
Yes, my name is Godot.

LUCILLE OUTBACK
Why, thank you. And what are you doing here?

GODOT
Waiting.

LUCILLE OUTBACK
Waiting? For whom?

GODOT
You.
(All-inclusive)

LUCILLE OUTBACK
What a treat.

GODOT
Some of it has been enjoyable.

MR. MALAPROP
Make a necessity of virtue.

LUCILLE OUTBACK
Only some?

GODOT
Not much.

LUCILLE OUTBACK
Then why? –

GODOT
It has kept me occupied, and I needed the instruction.

LUCILLE OUTBACK
How long? -

GODOT
Oh, here I have been at it a little more than five thousand years.

DANIEL
The dawn of civilization -

LUCILLE OUTBACK
Of man -

MR. MALAPROP
Of woman.
(GODOT smiles)

GODOT
I hope you are not going to spend the sixth millennium asking me questions about the previous five.

DANIEL
Why not? You could play Homer.

GODOT
I was Homer.
(Big pause)

MR. MALAPROP
I knew this was leading somewhere.

UNCLE STURTEVANT
Somewhere is here. Why do you only have one name?

GODOT
It is all I need, as you can see.

MR MALAPROP
Invention is the mother of necessity.

GODOT
Yes.

DANIEL
Well I hope you don't get sprung too soon.

GODOT
At your service, young man.

DANIEL
I need instruction more than you.

GODOT
You are not as old.

DANIEL
No.

GODOT
I can make an impression on you.

DANIEL
If I like.

GODOT
Yes. You will get it from the source. Ah, a nurse. I am rescued.
(NURSE takes GODOT's blood pressure, pulse, and temperature)

NURSE
Fine as always, Mr. Godot.
(GODOT smiles)

GODOT
I am healthy but I am here.

DANIEL
What brought you here?

GODOT
Five policemen and a fire truck.

DANIEL
Sounds exciting.

GODOT
I am sometimes flamboyant.

DANIEL
I love you.

GODOT
That was fast.

DANIEL
You are the father I never had.

GODOT
And the mother, too?

DANIEL
Yes.

GODOT
Well, aren't I the one?

MR. MALAPROP
And the two, too.

GODOT
I thought you had two fathers, A and B.

DANIEL
I am an orphan. They adopted me.

GODOT
So you are adopting me.

DANIEL
Yes.

UNCLE STURTEVANT
That makes sense. We should all choose our own parents.

DANIEL
What if I make a mistake?

GODOT
Correct it: choose again.

UNCLE STURTEVANT
Sounds like marriage.

MR. MALAPROP
Perfect makes practice.

GODOT
I rather like it here, with you.

LADY DALY
You wet-nosed lazy-bones. Get up. Gossip, gossip, gossip. You're worse than that T.V. You could make a living at it, sitting around here all day taking pills and drinking orange juice.

MR. MALAPROP
A sore eye for sight.

LADY DALY
You got it. Now who is going to help me clean up?
(Pause)

GODOT
That's my line.

LADY DALY
You're right about that, Mr. Godot. So you come over here with me...

DANIEL
Look at that.
(ALICE enters)

DANIEL
(Continued)
Hello, Ophelia.

ALICE
That is not my name.

UNCLE STURTEVANT
He was joking. How about helping clean up?
(ALICE sits down and stares at the ceiling)

UNCLE STURTEVANT
Oh.

DANIEL
We all need a rest. Besides, she's a member of the Royal Family.

UNCLE STURTEVANT
So that's why she's here. She was being hounded. It must have been her imagination.

DANIEL
Godot wasn't followed.

MR. MALAPROP
I was. It was a privilege.

ALICE
I have many privileges.

UNCLE STURTEVANT
And no responsibilities? Lady, you've lucked out.

ALICE
I like to dress well.
(All look at her dress, a purple ball-gown)

UNCLE STURTEVANT
Not bad. Whose party is it?

ALICE
This is my casual wear.

UNCLE STURTEVANT
Oh. Seems to me it would attract attention.

ALICE
I wear it everywhere.

UNCLE STURTEVANT
Even...?

ALICE
Yes. That is what ladies-in-waiting are for.

UNCLE STURTEVANT
I don't see –

ALICE
(Ignoring this)
Don't ask personal questions, please. The private functions of royalty are not of any interest to my subjects.

DANIEL
From what I read in the papers, you don't have many private functions left. Anyway, it's pretty obvious that even a queen uses the loo, and a princess -

ALICE
can be here. Yes. Well, let's not discuss it. It is very tiresome, just like you.

LADY DALY
Monsieur Godot, my humble apologies. I had no idea you could clean so well.

GODOT
I have lots of practice. It's a hobby.

LADY DALY
You want a job? I run an agency in my spare time. The good neighborhoods pay diddlypoop and the poor neighborhoods pay much better, don't ask me why.

GODOT
I guess it's a matter of personal pride.

LADY DALY
I guess that's your forte, too.

GODOT
How did you know?

LADY DALY
I know a few things, even if I look dumb.

GODOT
You look beautiful to me. And I won't disparage your brain, either.

LADY DALY
(Beaming)
Mr. Godot, you make me happy.

GODOT
And you, mi'lady, make me laugh.

LADY DALY
Call me Eleanor, sweetie.

GODOT
Yes, Eleanor, sweetie.

LADY DALY
Do you cook too?

GODOT
Sometimes I am the main course.

LADY DALY
I've been told human flesh is somewhat oily.

GODOT
My flesh is not exactly human, and there is enough of it to last indefinitely into the future.

UNCLE STURTEVANT
Cheap trick.

GODOT
Try me.

UNCLE STURTEVANT
(Pausing)
Maybe later.

LADY DALY
I don't have to try.

GODOT
I love the faithful. Unfortunately, most of them inhabit fantasy-land.

LADY DALY
And you are here -

GODOT
I am here.

LADY DALY
Oh.

GODOT
Now. What is for dinner?

ALICE
I'm having -

LADY DALY
You're having what we're having, and it ain't steak.

UNCLE STURTEVANT
Try franks and beans.

LADY DALY
My favorite.

GODOT
Mine, too.

LUCILLE OUTBACK
I would like mine medium rare.

GODOT
At your service.

LUCILLE OUTBACK
Cocktail parties are so fatiguing.

ALICE
The guests are nice.

LADY DALY
They're just as bad as anyone else, but better dressed.

DANIEL
No holes.

LUCILLE OUTBACK
(Yelling)
Don't tell me about gossip. It was all untrue.

LADY DALY
What was untrue?

LUCILLE OUTBACK
That I killed my first husband.
(She breaks down)

LADY DALY
Don't cry, or we'll need an umbrella. Here's a handkerchief. It's all I have, but it's for you.

LUCILLE OUTBACK
All you have?

LADY DALY
They cleaned my clock before I got here. I have nothing and no one.

LUCILLE OUTBACK
I like you.

LADY DALY
Thank you. I like you.

MR. MALAPROP
It's all bridge under the water.

LADY DALY
You said it.

LUCILLE OUTBACK
I am beginning to feel better.

GODOT
One more convert.

DANIEL
To what?

GODOT
Love. Humanity. Depth of soul. Understanding. You see what I mean?

DANIEL
You're a brick.

GODOT
Now don't be saying how wonderful I am. As soon as that begins, everybody starts asking for gifts. On the other hand, when things are going badly, they blame it all on me.

DANIEL
Then why do things go badly?

GODOT
Because I invented the devil.

DANIEL
And why – ?

GODOT
So I could acquire knowledge of evil without myself being or doing evil.

DANIEL
Then -

GODOT
The mess that men make of their lives is due to the devil or his disciples. That is all.

DANIEL
God!

GODOT
Godot!

DANIEL
Will it ever end?

GODOT
You will see.

DANIEL
And his disciples?

GODOT
You will see.

DANIEL
How do I know this is true?

GODOT
First look around you, and tell me what you think.

DANIEL
Eureka! I see a beginning.

GODOT
You are amusing.

DANIEL
So are you.

UNCLE STURTEVANT
I thought I was bad!

GODOT
The difference between us, Uncle Sturtevant, is that the weight of evidence is on my side.

UNCLE STURTEVANT
I am beginning to feel better.

GODOT
Relax. Enjoy yourself.

UNCLE STURTEVANT
Have you cured me?

GODOT
You have cured yourself. All you have to do is see the truth.

UNCLE STURTEVANT
How do you know it when you see it?

GODOT
You feel it - all the way inside. It is the poetry of the soul. It will feed you for a lifetime - for many lifetimes - once you have found it. And you, my dear uncle, have now found it.

UNCLE STURTEVANT
When can I leave here?

GODOT
There are rules. Follow them.

UNCLE STURTEVANT
Dear Mister Godot, I love you.

GODOT
You love yourself, that is why you love me.

(UNCLE STURTEVANT cries)

GODOT
Oh, please, I know you are happy. Anyways, a little megalomania never hurt anybody. It just made you look like a fool. And look at all the fools out there pretending they really are important. Well, they're not. And you are. What you have beats them down cold.

MR. MALAPROP
It's all dam under the water.

LADY DALY
Dinner, dinner, dinner. And I'm hungry, too.

(All inmates line up for trays of food, which they get and take to their seats around the room)
(DR. LANCE HABIT enters. Hidden under a distinguished, not to say imposing, exterior, he is a colossal nincompoop. He is one of those who has gotten to the right place the wrong way)

DR. LANCE HABIT
Well, well, well, are we having lunch?

LUCILLE OUTBACK
Hell, hell, hell, call it brunch.

LADY DALY
Have you had yours today, Dr. Habit?

(GODOT laughs)

DR. LANCE HABIT
Who laughed at me?

GODOT
I did, doctor. I apologize.

DR. LANCE HABIT
Troublemaker.

(All laugh)

DR. LANCE HABIT
Stop! Stop! Godot, you go to the quiet room. Miss Daly, I'll have you put in restraints if you don't shut up. For the rest of you - no grounds privileges till further notice.
(DR. LANCE HABIT leaves)

LADY DALY
I guess he's got pretty potent medicine for those with a sense of humor.

LUCILLE OUTBACK
He can cure everyone but himself.

ALICE
Godot could cure him.
(GODOT is silent)

LADY DALY
Godot is going to the quiet room.

LUCILLE OUTBACK
Solitary -

ALICE
Confinement.
(GODOT smiles)

LADY DALY
Mr. Godot, why do you smile?

GODOT
It will give me an opportunity to pray.

LADY DALY
To whom?

GODOT
The human race.

LADY DALY
Oh.

GODOT
Besides which, I'll fast. I need to lose some poundage, anyways.

LUCILLE OUTBACK
Poor Godot.

MR. MALAPROP
You will be the former self of your shadow.

GODOT
All set-backs are opportunities in disguise.

MR. MALAPROP
All opportunities are setbacks in disguise.

GODOT
Dear Mr. Malaprop, what would we do without your wisdom?

MR. MALAPROP
Eat liver?

ALICE
Yuck.

LADY DALY
Blacks like me like liver. It's cheap and nutritious.

ALICE
I am neither cheap nor nutritious.

LUCILLE OUTBACK
We know you aren't nutritious, my dear. We weren't planning to eat you.

ALICE
Just in case.

LUCILLE OUTBACK
Oh. Well if they give me your liver, I'll see that a suitable donee is found.

DANIEL
By then she'll be smothered in onions.

LUCILLE OUTBACK
My poodle likes liver.

ALICE
Liver, liver, liver! What about getting Godot out of the quiet room?

DANIEL
He seems to like it there. One mattress on the floor, a bare bulb in the ceiling that is always on, and no conveniences. Spartan, I would say.

ALICE
But he's a great personage!

DANIEL
He is great because he is small.

MR. MALAPROP
He is small because he is great.

UNCLE STURTEVANT
We should be like him.

LADY DALY
Let us all be small.
(All laugh, as LADY DALY is quite large)
(Enter DR. LANCE HABIT)

DR. LANCE HABIT
Who is laughing?
(Silence)

DR. LANCE HABIT
(Continued)
Lady Daly, come here. Are you the culprit?

LADY DALY
It's beginning to look like it.

DR. LANCE HABIT
Then you get into quiet room #2. Now!
(She exits)

DR. LANCE HABIT
Any other takers?
(Silence)

DR. LANCE HABIT
(Continued)
Good. You all need discipline, and that's what you'll get. Goodbye.
(DR. LANCE HABIT marches out)

LUCILLE OUTBACK
We have lost our two best lights.
(DOTTIE DUMPLING appearing)

DOTTIE DUMPLING
The dirt here is appalling. I can see Dr. Habit has been around.

LUCILLE OUTBACK
How can you tell?

DOTTIE DUMPLING
Simple. It smells of cigarettes, and patients aren't allowed to smoke.

LUCILLE OUTBACK
A new Sherlock Holmes.

DOTTIE DUMPLING
My name is Dottie Dumpling, and I clean.

DANIEL
Pleased to meet you - I speak for us all.

DOTTIE DUMPLING
You are all very charming.
(Everyone smiles)

DOTTIE DUMPLING
(Continued)
All smiles. Now we can't all be that sick, can we?
(Fewer smiles around)

DOTTIE DUMPLING
(Continued)
Look at my name. First: Dottie. And I'm not Dotty. Second: Dumpling, and I'm thin.

MR. MALAPROP
Don't judge a cover by its book!

DOTTIE DUMPLING
You got it.

A
Then what are we doing here?

DOTTIE DUMPLING
You are just visiting, as is Monsieur Malaprop. The rest of you are involved in some kind of severe imbroglio.

DANIEL
When they admitted me, they said I was suffering from sexual compulsions.

DOTTIE DUMPLING
Nonsense. You're twenty and you're horny. You don't need this place. You need a girl.

ALICE
Well!

DOTTIE DUMPLING
Sorry. I try not to offend, but I didn't know you could overhear.

ALICE
I am a princess of the blood. I never overhear.

UNCLE STURTEVANT
Here they take your blood every day, and they don't care what you hear.

ALICE
Not that blood. My lineage.

UNCLE STURTEVANT
So you have a history. The doctors will be glad to know. How many times have you been in one of these places?

ALICE
(Huffily)
This is my first.

UNCLE STURTEVANT
I suggest you take it for all it's worth. Then you won't have to expand your lineage.

ALICE
I will never come again. It is too humiliating.

MR. MALAPROP
Don't cry. My brain doesn't work either. Life is such.

ALICE
Such what?

UNCLE STURTEVANT
I shall take care of everything.

MR. MALAPROP
The oyster is his world.

ALICE
I am getting confused.

UNCLE STURTEVANT
Declare yourself! Who are you??

ALICE
I don't know. I thought -

MR. MALAPROP
A thought for your pennies.

ALICE
I don't belong here. I am a Princess.

DANIEL
I think, like the rest of us, you have earned a little relaxation from the world.

UNCLE STURTEVANT
Hear, hear.

DOTTIE DUMPLING
I don't hear anything.
(Listening)

ALICE
I think I am going crazy.

UNCLE STURTEVANT
It gets worse.

MR. MALAPROP
It gets better before it gets worse.

ALICE
Hell! Oh, excuse me.

DOTTIE DUMPLING
Here comes Godot, out of the quiet room.

GODOT
Me voici.

ALICE
Enchantée.

MR. MALAPROP
Plus c'est la même chose, plus ça change.
(LADY DALY entering)

LADY DALY
Cut the friggin' French. You ain't a frog.

UNCLE STURTEVANT
How was your stay, Mr. Godot?

GODOT
Very relaxing. You can look at a bare light bulb for hours and not be blinded, quite unlike the sun.

DANIEL
What did you see in this light?

GODOT
A little warmth.

ALICE
Unintended, I promise.

GODOT
Who knows what is ever intended? I look at results. And the result here is that I am back with you, minus a few hours sleep.

DANIEL
No thoughts to share?

GODOT
The light was warm.

DANIEL
But you were locked in.

GODOT
I still am. Only now I have a slightly greater range. I think I shall organize the patients.

UNCLE STURTEVANT
What a novel thought.

GODOT
Not at all. I believe "organization" is a tool of Leninism.

DANIEL
Good God, you're not a follower of Lenin?

GODOT
(Laughing)
Of course not. He was a child of the devil. I just thought we should join hands and see what we can do for ourselves - and others.

DOTTIE DUMPLING
How do you mean, Mr. Godot?

GODOT
Well, you all agree you love me?
(All nod)

GODOT
(Continued)
Yet you don't know who I am?
(All nod)

GODOT
(Continued)
Do you hear what I say?
(Some nod)

GODOT
(Continued)
Can you see what I do?
(Fewer nod)

GODOT
(Continued)
And how many wish to do likewise?
(Silence. No nods)

GODOT
(Continued)
(Smiles)
Ahh. I am not so popular as I had thought. Habit – not the Doctor but the thing – has a pretty strong grip on people. We shall have to see what we can do to change that.

ALICE
I don't want to change.

UNCLE STURTEVANT
Nor I.

LUCILLE OUTBACK
Nor I.
(General agreement on this point)

GODOT
I see that Doctor Habit will have to be a pretty good therapist if any of you is ever to get out of here.

LUCILLE OUTBACK
He gives us pills.

GODOT
Ah, pills. Is that good?

UNCLE STURTEVANT
They control my megalomania.

LUCILLE OUTBACK
And my paranoia.

LADY DALY
And my aggression.

GODOT
Fantastic. And these pills, do they keep you cured?

LADY DALY
Oh, yes, if you continue to take them.

GODOT
If not?

LUCILLE OUTBACK
You wind up back here.

GODOT
Too bad.
(Everyone agrees it is too bad)

GODOT
(Continued)
I think I shall have to come up with a supplement.

UNCLE STURTEVANT
To what?

GODOT
Your pills.

UNCLE STURTEVANT
Nonsense. Anyway, I am a Sturtevant, descended directly from Peter Stuyvesant, and I don't need pills.

GODOT
Come here.

UNCLE STURTEVANT
Why?

GODOT
I want to look into your eye, close-up.

UNCLE STURTEVANT
Here. What do you see?

GODOT
Pain.

UNCLE STURTEVANT
Phooey.

GODOT
Discord and a faithless son.
(UNCLE STURTEVANT begins to tremble, a little at first, then as dialogue proceeds, violently)

GODOT
(Continued)
Have you wished to kill?
(UNCLE STURTEVANT is silent)

GODOT
(Continued)
Are you afraid of yourself?
(UNCLE STURTEVANT shakes violently)

GODOT
(Continued)
You do not need pills. You need love, including the love you threw away on your son.

UNCLE STURTEVANT
Oh, God.

GODOT
No, Godot. At least get my name right.
(Smiles all around)

DR. LANCE HABIT
(Entering)
What's going on here?

A
Since I am only a visitor, I shall speak for what I have seen.

Godot here has cured Uncle Sturtevant of his megalomania by putting a mirror up to the face of his own tragedy.

GODOT
Uncle Sturtevant has been wounded in his heart. I have helped to make him better.

DR. LANCE HABIT
Nonsense. Uncle Sturtevant will get better when I say so, not before. I am the Doctor, not you, Mr. Godot, or anyone else.

A
I am a witness –

DR. LANCE HABIT
You are a visitor and nothing else. So visit and then leave.

(A shuts up)
(DR. LANCE HABIT leaves)

MR. MALAPROP
A rose is a rose.

ALICE
Gertrude Stein goes both ways indiscriminately!

GODOT
I think she only went one way - and that was alright.

DANIEL
I like girls.

GODOT
Don't protest too much or we'll begin to wonder.
(DANIEL loses face)

GODOT
(Continued)
Well, well, well, you'll be out of here soon, diagnosis, pills and all, and then you can have as many girlfriends as you please. There is no shortage of girls, only of time, and you are young – and I am not.

DANIEL
How old are you?

GODOT
As old as this earth. In fact, older. This is just my most recent incarnation.

A
If you said such things outside, they would lock you up.
(GODOT gestures: here I am)

A
Oh.

LUCILLE OUTBACK
I will put you up for a club when we get out.

GODOT
But you are a woman, and you club is single - sex.

LUCILLE OUTBACK
Well, my husband will put you up for his club.

GODOT
But it is exclusionary, and I am by nature inclusive.

LUCILLE OUTBACK
Don't be difficult. Everybody is entitled to have his own circle of friends.

MR. MALAPROP
Choose and pick, choose and pick.

GODOT
What if you like everybody?

UNCLE STURTEVANT
What if everybody likes you?

GODOT
It would be hard to justify exclusivity in that case.

LUCILLE OUTBACK
This is too much for me.
(Lies back in a chair)
I don't mean to do anyone harm.

GODOT
The only one you harm is yourself. Open up your life, it will make more than yourself happy.

LUCILLE OUTBACK
Oh, I am feeling better. The paranoia seems to be lifting.

GODOT
You can say goodbye to it, Lucille. You are free of your presumptions.

DR. LANCE HABIT
(Walking in)
Will you stop curing people, Mr. Godot? That is my province, not yours. While you're at it, you might try curing yourself.

GODOT
What is wrong with me, Doctor?

DR. LANCE HABIT
You are a manic-depressive with paranoid affect. You sit in flower-beds, you speak in non-sequiturs, you stop traffic in the middle of Times Square, you walk through Harlem at eleven at night, and through Central Park at twelve, you hike from Battery Park to Yonkers in your socks when it is raining, and so on. Is this normal?

GODOT
It is playful, and definitely not normal. But it had its purpose.

DR. LANCE HABIT
And what was that?

GODOT
To hone my will, and to focus your attention, both of which I have done.

DR. LANCE HABIT
(Furious)
I shall prescribe some thorazine for you tomorrow morning. You are obviously out of control.

GODOT
You are the one who is out of control, Doctor. I have always known what I was doing.

DR. LANCE HABIT
You are a fraud, Mr. Godot!

GODOT
And you are a Doctor, Dr. Habit. I hope there are not many like you.

DR. LANCE HABIT
Quiet! Or I shall put you in seclusion.
(GODOT says nothing. His face becomes impassive)

DR. LANCE HABIT
Oh!
(DR. LANCE HABIT exits)

LADY DALY
He reminds me of my boyfriend. Dr. Godot - I mean Mr. Godot - when they bite, you bite back.

GODOT
One day in seclusion is enough for now, Lady Daly. But if we all - all of us - bite back, some good may come of it.

ALICE
Oh, Mr. Godot!

GODOT
An admirer already.

ALICE
Don't you love me?

GODOT
I am spread pretty thin at the moment.

ALICE
I'll wait.

GODOT
But I'm not royal, not even noble.

ALICE
I can arrange things.

GODOT
Why not you become a commoner? All you have to do is renounce your title.

ALICE
Renounce my title!? It is all I have!

GODOT
Not at all. You are attractive and talented and moderately intelligent. Even without a title you would have a lineage.

ALICE
But I would have to earn a living.

GODOT
Worse things can happen. Anyhow, a title is a burden. It involves you in a whole hypocritical charade of trying to be what you are not - human. Well, throw it out the window and assume your humanity. Then you can be whatever you are. I am certainly no prince and have no desire to be.

ALICE
Oh, Mr. Godot, my title is myself. I cannot give it up.

GODOT
As you choose. I cannot choose for you. I can only help you see what the possibilities are.

MR. MALAPROP
Mr. Godot, why are we mad?

GODOT
I suppose some of us are sick. Illness comes in many forms, and this is one of them. Why, for the present, I cannot say. But you will learn why soon enough.

A
Daniel, why are you here?

DANIEL
It is someone's sorry joke.

A
But are you ill?

DANIEL
I don't think so. At least I didn't feel ill till they started treating me. Now I feel wretched.

A
We'll get you out of here in no time.

DANIEL
Try.

A
Where is that Doctor Habit? What an awful name.

DANIEL
There are nice doctors, but mine is Habit.

A
What's his first name?

DANIEL
Lance.

MR. MALAPROP
There's a name in nothing.

A
I should say there are lots of names in nothing.

DANIEL
God knows what parents will cook up.

A
You don't look sick.

DANIEL
Looks are not very reliable in this department.

A
You seem coherent.

DANIEL
Ask me how I feel.

A
How do you feel?

DANIEL
Crazy. I am being followed, my mail is opened, my apartment is bugged, my pills are poisoned, my shower scalds at odd moments, rumors about me float all over New York, - none of them true - my private life is made public, my poetry is constantly rejected on the weakest of pretexts, those who know me collude; in short, my entire life has slipped out of my control.

A
Now I see why you are here. Is any of this true?

DANIEL
You tell me.

A
Well, I don't think so. But finding evidence for what you say could not be easy.

DANIEL
Impossible.

A
Then let's leave it alone and proceed from here.

DANIEL
Yes?

A
How long have you been here?

DANIEL
Two weeks.

A
You'll need at least another two to get out.

DANIEL
Remember, my doctor is Habit.

A
Give it another four weeks.

DANIEL
Eeeow!

A
Your problems are not minor.

DANIEL
I shouldn't have said anything. It always gets me in trouble.

A
Oh, Daniel, I wish so much to help you. If you do what the doctor says, you'll be out soon.

DANIEL
That Doctor?

A
Do you have another?

DANIEL
Saints preserve me.

GODOT
I suppose they will.

DANIEL
Mr. Godot, am I going to die?

GODOT
(Laughs)
Daniel, we are all going to die. The question is, then what?

DANIEL
Well?

GODOT
Those who have made the right choices will continue to live here or elsewhere, as one thing or another; those who have made the wrong choices will be reduced to nothing.

DANIEL
Nothing?

GODOT
Nothing.

DANIEL
But what is nothing?

GODOT
Nothing does not exist.

DANIEL
Oh.

GODOT
Think about it.

DANIEL
I'll try.

GODOT
You'll succeed. Any other questions?
(There are none)

GODOT
(Continued)
I wish all my assignments were so easy.

ALICE
But this is a mental hospital.

GODOT
Yes.

ALICE
Oh.

GODOT
Life – parents, friends, guardians – have softened you up for the kill.

ALICE
And we were killed.

GODOT
Exactly. And here I am trying to bring you back into life. You may have made foolish choices, but you were never wicked.

LADY DALY
What next?

GODOT
I suppose they'll patch you up and send you on out to get knocked down again.

LUCILLE OUTBACK
I have a social worker.

GODOT
A band-aid on a severe wound to the head.

LADY DALY
Then what are we supposed to do?

MR. MALAPROP
Easy go as easy come.

GODOT
Monsieur Malaprop, you are a dream.
(MR. MALAPROP tips his hat)

GODOT
(Continued)
I am trying to think of a plan of action that will redeem us all. But, then, I never do anything premeditated.

LUCILLE OUTBACK
Never?

GODOT
Well, hardly ever.

UNCLE STURTEVANT
And he is hardly ever sick at sea.

GODOT
I never go to sea.

UNCLE STURTEVANT
All the better. You can be sick here.

GODOT
Here I am.

LADY DALY
But you are not sick.

GODOT
Words, words, words:
So you think you are tough?
You are going to make me unhappy?
You are going to beat me up?
I have a better idea than you.
I shall think you into a pit,
Where a black lantern will be lit,
Shining on your frightened eyes,
And no one will pay attention
To your cries;
I shall put your hat on you ass-
Backwards, and make you walk
Cross-legged like a crow
Into a road full of trucks,
Which will run on your toes,
Crushing them. O, joy!
Punishment for my pain!
Vindication of shame!
Will you ever try,
You black-eared toad,
To knock me down again?
Even I can play a tune or two.

ALICE
That was very good, Mr. Godot. I wish I could write like that.

LADY DALY
I wish I could speak like that.

GODOT
You can. Just listen to yourself.

LADY DALY
Fellow citizens of the World, rescue yourselves from the forces of Impotence. Steal back your lives! Turn the tables on adversity! Find love where it does not lie! You are free to wish what you want and then to make it come true. Help yourselves – no one else knows how, as well as you. I love you all!

GODOT
Lady Daly, I could not have said it better. You were born with a silver spoon in your mouth.

LADY DALY
But I am a black overweight manic-depressive.

GODOT
You are my friend, and I am your audience whenever you need one.

LADY DALY
Oh, Mr. Godot, I fail you at every turn.

GODOT
No, you are successful whenever you exercise your will. Just do so in the right direction, and marvels will appear.

LUCILLE OUTBACK
Oh, Mr. Godot…

GODOT
Yes!

LUCILLE OUTBACK
May I be good, too?

GODOT
This is not an exclusive club.

MR. MALAPROP
Read David Copperfield.

UNCLE STURTEVANT
Or Shakespeare.

GODOT
Whatever.

LADY DALY
You mean no one is excluded from happiness?

GODOT
Of course not. That would serve no purpose except to play into the hands of the forces of evil.

UNCLE STURTEVANT
Ahh!

GODOT
Please close your mouth, Uncle Sturtevant. I am not a dentist.

UNCLE STURTEVANT
Well I am, and you perform the most delicate extractions in the most artful way.

GODOT
I am an artist in my spare time.

LUCILLE OUTBACK
Oh, what kind?

GODOT
Performance artist.

LUCILLE OUTBACK
I haven't heard of that.

GODOT
It blossomed in the sixties. Now it's a bit passé, but I keep my end up.

LUCILLE OUTBACK
May I watch you sometime?

GODOT
You are.

LUCILLE OUTBACK
Oh, this is fascinating.

GODOT
It's work, and I am glad to have it.

LUCILLE OUTBACK
So many actors are out of work.

GODOT
The theatrical profession is under-utilized. I wonder why?

UNCLE STURTEVANT
Supply and demand.

LUCILLE OUTBACK
Gross commercialization.

ALICE
Exploitation.

MR. MALAPROP
I think we are all being ridden for a take.

GODOT
Ah, Mr. Malaprop, right again.
(They bow to one another)

GODOT
Yes, and art is hard.

ALICE
Ars longa, vita brevis.

GODOT
That would be a good one for Mr. Malaprop.

ALICE
He doesn't know Latin.

GODOT
How do you?

ALICE
I may be a princess, but I have a brain.

GODOT
At last. Now we know your problem.

ALICE
You're right! I feel better already. Oh, Mr. Godot, thank you.

GODOT
Thank yourself. Everyone here has the wherewithal to cure themselves. It is a matter of will properly directed. Just think, you may all set yourselves free!

ALL
Oh, Mr. Godot, we love you.

GODOT
Let's keep it quiet. Habit may reappear.

ALICE
Habit or habit?

GODOT
Either one; they're both deadly.

ALICE
Oh.

UNCLE STURTEVANT
But what if we can't stick to our new régime?

GODOT
You want an instant replay?
(*All say no*)
Thank you. You get what you ask for.

DANIEL
Then how do we get out of here?

GODOT
You are well. Just behave, and they'll let you go. After all, though Dr. Habit runs the place, not even he can keep you here if you're demonstrably cured.

LADY DALY
Oh, Mr. Godot. You are a peach!

DANIEL
Yes, Mr. Godot, but you are here, and it seems you have always been well.

GODOT
I have my moments.

DOTTIE DUMPLING
Of inspiration.

GODOT
I have my slack times, too. Right now, I am resting.

DANIEL
I wonder what you're like when you're at work?

GODOT
Dazzling.

LADY DALY
We can't wait.

GODOT
As I say, I am resting. After that...?

LADY DALY
After that we put you on a float in Macy's Thanksgiving Day Parade.

GODOT
That's a bit conspicuous. I might become a target for the world's malcontents.

DANIEL
Amongst others.

GODOT
Let us tread softly, and watch out for other peoples' toes.

LADY DALY
You aren't any fun.

GODOT
Be patient, Lady Daly. We will have fun, but we must get our timing right.

DANIEL
Otherwise, all is for naught.

GODOT
There you are.

ACT II

SCENE 1

Same scene, some two weeks later.

    LUCILLE OUTBACK
I thought we were going to be at home by now.

    UNCLE STURTEVANT
Me too. I think someone is conspiring to keep us here.

    LUCILLE OUTBACK
Wait. I'm paranoid.

    UNCLE STURTEVANT
And I'm in charge.

    LUCILLE OUTBACK
Then you must know why we're all still here.

    MR. MALAPROP
Better never than late.

    LUCILLE OUTBACK
What does that mean?

    UNCLE STURTEVANT
He's always wrong - or right - I don't know which.

    DANIEL
Mr. Godot, why are we still here?

GODOT

Because in your present state you would not last more than five minutes outside.

UNCLE STURTEVANT

I feel well.

DANIEL

Me, too.

GODOT

That is no indication of your state of health. You must be up and about, go for walks through the gardens, cook, sing, play dominoes or ping pong, and so on. And you must talk to your doctor and help him to understand what's troubling you, what brought you here. When they know that, then you will be on your way home.

DOTTIE DUMPLING

I don't want to go home.

LADY DALY

Don't worry, Dottie, you can come live with me.

DOTTIE DUMPLING

I want my job back.

GODOT

I am sure you will have it back, Dottie. The doctor's methods may seem harsh, but in fact they perform miracles. I am sure you will be back to work soon.

LADY DALY

How do you know that?

GODOT

What was I supposed to say?

LADY DALY

Oh.

GODOT
I cannot wish us all out of here. That would just put us all out in the street with the same problems that bedevil us here. Our stay would have been for nothing.

MR. MALAPROP
Nothing is as nothing does.

GODOT
It is just like life: if we do not ask the right questions, we do not get the right answers.

DANIEL
What is the right question?

GODOT
Well?

LADY DALY
Why we are here?

GODOT
And?

DANIEL
To discover what it is we do not know.

GODOT
And then you will be prepared.

LADY DALY
For what?

GODOT
For what comes on the other side of life.

DANIEL
What if you're not ready?

GODOT
Then you have another go round.

LADY DALY
And another and another -

DANIEL
Until you learn your lesson.

UNCLE STURTEVANT
Sounds vaguely Asiatic to me.

GODOT
Uncle Sturtevant, you are a winner.

UNCLE STURTEVANT
Always thought so.

MR. MALAPROP
Mother is the necessity of invention.

GODOT
I am not so sure. Anyway, right now we must cooperate.

LUCILLE OUTBACK
Collaborate.

LADY DALY
Give in.

DANIEL
Capitulate.

ALICE
Quit.

MR. MALAPROP
Lance, Dr. Habit.
(Enter DR. HABIT with some STUDENT DOCTORS and some NURSES)

DR. LANCE HABIT
Time for a community meeting.
(All move chairs in semi-circle facing audience)

DR. LANCE HABIT
(Continued)
Let us begin. To begin with, I have bad news. Douglas Pinckney, who left us two weeks ago, has committed suicide.
(Silence)

DR. LANCE HABIT
(Continued)
Does no one have a reaction?
(Silence)

DR. LANCE HABIT
(Continued)
Well, for those of you in a similar position, I would point out that shifting the burden of guilt onto the shoulders of those who survive you will not work. Some of us may grieve, but we all eventually get on with our lives.

UNCLE STURTEVANT
Dr. Habit, we do not kill ourselves to inspire guilt in others or in you. We do it because we are in pain, and there is no other way out.

LADY DALY
We are not here because we want to punish someone, except perhaps ourselves.

ALICE
I am here because of a failure in love.

DR. LANCE HABIT
Good cause for pain, my dear.

ALICE
You know nothing about pain, Dr. Habit.

LADY DALY
So shut up.

DR. LANCE HABIT
Miss Daly –

LADY DALY
Lady to you.

DR. LANCE HABIT
Lady Daly, you must control yourself, or you will be back in the quiet room.

LADY DALY
Appropriate.

DR. LANCE HABIT
I warn you.

GODOT
And pain, Dr. Habit, where does this pain come from?

DR. LANCE HABIT
I suppose from experience.

GODOT
Then why are some here and some not?

DR. LANCE HABIT
Because some of us know how to protect ourselves.

GODOT
Do you teach that here?

DR. LANCE HABIT
Health is the best preventative.

GODOT
Very good. Do you know pain, Dr. Habit?

DR. LANCE HABIT
I think so.

GODOT
Ah. It is hard to teach what one does not know.
(*Silence*)

GODOT
(Continued)
Mrs. Outback, why are you here?

LUCILLE OUTBACK
I am afraid.

GODOT
Again? I thought we had cured you.

LUCILLE OUTBACK
I am having a relapse.

GODOT
You will certainly engage Dr. Habit for a while.

LUCILLE OUTBACK
I have. And it is time for me to go.

GODOT
But has Dr. Habit freed you of your fears?

LUCILLE OUTBACK
No. He has added to them.

GODOT
How?

LUCILLE OUTBACK
Now I am afraid of him.

GODOT
How helpful. How did he do this?

LUCILLE OUTBACK
He prescribed an overdose of medications for me.

GODOT
Why?

LUCILLE OUTBACK
Because he was afraid of me.

GODOT
And why should he be afraid of you? Why should anybody be afraid of you?

LUCILLE OUTBACK
Because I know.

GODOT
Know?

LUCILLE OUTBACK
Things.

GODOT
Things?
(Silence)

GODOT
(Continued)
Well, we'll leave the rest up to your medical team, and they can discuss it with Dr. Habit, who no doubt has lots to say.

LADY DALY
Life is so fatiguing.

GODOT
Why is that, Lady Daly?

LADY DALY
I barely sleep, because my roommate is always spying on me.

GODOT
Is paranoia part of your diagnosis?

LADY DALY
I don't know, but she is spying.

GODOT
We'll have to talk to the nurses.

LADY DALY
If you can find one that is not spying. I'll look into it for you. Now, what brought you here?

LADY DALY
Mania. I beat up my boyfriend.

GODOT
I guess he's not as big as you.

LADY DALY
He's a punk, but I love him.

GODOT
Then why did you beat him up?

LADY DALY
He was out of line.

GODOT
Seems reasonable. Did you tell anyone here?

LADY DALY
When I was admitted, yes.

GODOT
Something seems to have been lost in the transmission. You should talk to your doctors. I think you are supposed to be manic.

LADY DALY
I take my pills.

GODOT
Well, you seem alright to me. Talk to your team.

LADY DALY
Team, team, what's a team?

LUCILLE OUTBACK
Honey, those are the people that look after you here.

LADY DALY
Well, I hope they let me go home soon.

GODOT
So do we.

DR. LANCE HABIT
I think our community meeting has been hijacked.

GODOT
Excuse me.

DR. LANCE HABIT
Does anyone other than Mr. Godot care to ask a question?

DOTTIE DUMPLING
Yes. Why do you dislike us?
(DR. LANCE HABIT at a loss)

DOTTIE DUMPLING
Is it because we are black or Hispanic or simply people of no means?

DR. LANCE HABIT
Nonsense. I do like you, I am very fond of you.

LUCILLE OUTBACK
Then why are you so autocratic?

DR. LANCE HABIT
I didn't realize…

LUCILLE OUTBACK
Well, now you do.

ALICE
You are not helping us.

LUCILLE OUTBACK
You make my paranoia worse.

UNCLE STURTEVANT
With you around, I have to think I'm God just to protect myself. You may think I like it, but I don't. I would rather be anything than God.

DR. LANCE HABIT
I am sorry.

(Silence)

MR. MALAPROP
All ends well that is well.

A
Well, I'm well and I want to get out of here.

DR. LANCE HABIT
What are your symptoms?

DANIEL
He's with me.

DR. LANCE HABIT
Oh.

DANIEL
He's one of my fathers.

DR. LANCE HABIT
How many do you have?

A
Two. Me and Mr. Malaprop.

DANIEL
Oh! B! You here too!

MR. MALAPROP
It's hard to understand, but very easy to believe.

DR. LANCE HABIT
I'm going crazy.

GODOT
Reality looks like that sometimes.

MR. MALAPROP
You look like the canary that ate the cat.

GODOT
So we all do.
(General merriment)

GODOT
(To DR. LANCE HABIT)
Well?

DR. LANCE HABIT
You are all discharged!
(Everyone dances)

ACT II

SCENE 2

The gardens outside the hospital. It is September and sunny and very beautiful. The former patients are out for a stroll. It is at least a month since they were "discharged."

DANIEL
Funny. I always wanted to leave. Now I want to stay.

LUCILLE OUTBACK
There is no staff. When Dr. Habit discharged us, there was no reason for them to stay.

LADY DALY
Now we have a home, a nice home.

DOTTIE DUMPLING
For free.

GODOT
We must keep it up, or it will fall down.

ALICE
We don't want that to happen.

GODOT
So long as we stay here, it won't.

ALICE
I am applying for a job in town.

UNCLE STURTEVANT
What job?

ALICE
As a waitress.

UNCLE STURTEVANT
Are you crazy! You're a princess.

ALICE
Mr. Godot said that titles are empty labels, and I agree. To be a princess does not guarantee you are good, or anything else, I think.

LADY DALY
My name is Lady, and we know I live up to it.

ALICE
Well I could not live up to being a princess, so I have quit.

UNCLE STURTEVANT
And now you're a waitress.
(He laughs)

LUCILLE OUTBACK
I like to think I'm somebody.

LADY DALY
You are, but around here it doesn't count for much.

ALICE
Maybe you should be a waitress, too, Lucille.

LUCILLE OUTBACK
What does it pay?

ALICE
It depends on the tips. If you are polite and kind without being forward, you will be rewarded.

LUCILLE OUTBACK
Oh. Well -

ALICE
I'll take you down tomorrow. I'm sure they have room.

GODOT
Uncle Sturtevant!

UNCLE STURTEVANT
Yes.

GODOT
Still musing over immortality?

UNCLE STURTEVANT
Yes. And the Greatness of Being.

GODOT
Heavy - duty.

UNCLE STURTEVANT
Yes.

GODOT
Where does it all lead?

UNCLE STURTEVANT
Into the dark.

GODOT
Do you see in the dark?

UNCLE STURTEVANT
That is what I have been trying to do for some time now.

GODOT
How do you get out?

UNCLE STURTEVANT
By finding my courage.

GODOT
Yes?

UNCLE STURTEVANT
It is hard to live with the truth about yourself. Sometimes it seems easier just to run away.

GODOT
But it is not easier, is it?

UNCLE STURTEVANT
No. I cannot run away forever. A little pain now saves a lot of pain later.

GODOT
You cannot lie to yourself forever.

UNCLE STURTEVANT
I am tired of lies. I want my life back.

GODOT
Then you will have it. And your brain, too. Look at me. I am the one you are seeking. Can you tell?

UNCLE STURTEVANT
Yes. The truth is in your eyes, whenever I look.

GODOT
I am only Godot, and you see right through me.

UNCLE STURTEVANT
(Breaking down)
Oh, Mr. Godot, I don't see how I can do without you, without somebody. I am so alone.

GODOT
So am I.
(GODOT looks very sad)

UNCLE STURTEVANT
You, alone?

GODOT
More so than anyone else.
(UNCLE STURTEVANT is blowing his nose)

GODOT
(Continued)
Feel better?

UNCLE STURTEVANT
Yes. Mr. Godot, who are you?

GODOT
It is difficult to say, and for now inappropriate to discuss.

UNCLE STURTEVANT
How can anyone live without you?
(GODOT gestures around himself)

GODOT
Things seem to be improving from what they were.

ALICE
I wonder why.

MR. MALAPROP
Mother is the necessity of invention.

GODOT
It is not mere invention, Mr. Malaprop. People have begun to do the right thing.

LUCILLE OUTBACK
We are setting ourselves free.

DOTTIE DUMPLING
Of what?

LUCILLE OUTBACK
Past injury.

DANIEL
Yes, now even I have a future to live for.

A & B
And we can still live for each other and set Daniel free.

LUCILLE OUTBACK
I feel so invigorated. I think I shall go out and chop down a tree.

UNCLE STURTEVANT
I'll help. But make sure it's not cherry. We want history behind us – and our future ahead.

GODOT
It seems to be a little damp out here.

MR. MALAPROP
Rain is right.

GODOT
I suppose it is. I am beginning to feel very weak. My will seems to be softening, and my sight shows me nothing. Now I am no more than human.

DANIEL
Mr. Godot, what is wrong?

GODOT
Nothing is wrong, Daniel. It is just that I have done my good deed, and now I have become what I had chosen to be.

DANIEL
What is that?

GODOT
A man.

LADY DALY
Oh, Mr. Godot!

GODOT
That is all I am now, and just as vulnerable as the rest of you.

DOTTIE DUMPLING
You still give good advice.

GODOT
Now it is up to you to give good advice, even to yourselves. You have seen me in action, now go out and practice it.

MR. MALAPROP
Preach what you practice.

GODOT
That, too, Mr. Malaprop. The right word can often save a situation.

DOTTIE DUMPLING
How can we save yours, Mr. Godot?

GODOT
Save yourselves and I shall be saved. That is all I can say. Now I must go. We all have a little housecleaning to do, even me. Oh, God.

(GODOT falls on the ground in front of the entire cast and begins to have convulsion. At the same time he calls out:)

I love you, I love you, I love you.

(The convulsions grow more intense until GODOT is screaming in agony and still repeating "I love you". Finally, there is a peak in his pain and the convulsions subside and GODOT falls silent. Everyone present is amazed, but not embarrassed)

Ohhh.

DOTTIE DUMPING
Are you alright, Mr. Godot?

GODOT
Yes, Dottie. Are you?

DOTTIE DUMPLING
Oh, yes, Mr. Godot. I was afraid you would die. Did you?

GODOT
No, Dottie. I am still alive. But I think there is one less personage present amongst our number.

DOTTIE DUMPLING
Who is that, Mr. Godot?

GODOT
The devil.

(Much attention given to this by witnesses)

GODOT
I have taken him back to where he came from.

A
Where is that, Mr. Godot?

GODOT
To nothing. He has been reduced to nothing.

A
Then what is left?

GODOT
A mess. Each one of us must clean up his mess.

MR. MALAPROP
"If everyone swept his own threshold, the world would be clean." Goethe.

DOTTIE DUMPLING
After that, Mr. Godot?

GODOT
After that, Dottie, we really are in Heaven.

DOTTIE DUMPLING
Oh, Mr. Godot!

(All present swarm around GODOT)

ACT III

SCENE 1

As in Act I, some months later.

    DANIEL
I wonder what has become of Dr. Habit?

    GODOT
He is hanging from a large apple tree in the patients' orchard.

    DANIEL
Suicide?
(GODOT nods yes)

    DANIEL
(Continued)
Wonder who diagnosed him?

    GODOT
It was a self-diagnosis.

    DANIEL
I guess it was accurate.

    GODOT
Yes.

    DANIEL
What about the other doctors and nurses?

GODOT
I think they survived the liberation.

DANIEL
But they're not here?

GODOT
No. It was not congenial to them.

DANIEL
And the patients?

GODOT
They come and go.

DANIEL
Yes.
(Some patients come and go)

GODOT
Do you know who I am?

DANIEL
You are Godot.

GODOT
Yes. But do you know who Godot is?

DANIEL
Of course.

GODOT
And I don't frighten you?

DANIEL
No. I like you.

GODOT
I like you.

DANIEL
Yes.

GODOT
I am older than you.

DANIEL
It doesn't show.

GODOT
No. I am even older than your father.

DANIEL
It doesn't show.

GODOT
I like you very much.

DANIEL
Me, too.
(They kiss once lightly, then once passionately)

DANIEL
(Continued)
What are all the women going to say?

GODOT
They know what it means to have a man.

DANIEL
Have you ever loved a woman?

GODOT
Of course.

DANIEL
Then -

GODOT
This is a first for me.

DANIEL
Me, too. I wonder what A and B will say.

UNCLE STURTEVANT
Any room for me?

GODOT
Monogamy is the best policy. That excludes you.

UNCLE STURTEVANT
Isn't it the way. I guess I'll have to try one of the ladies.

DOTTIE DUMPLING
(Looking alluring)
Hello, Uncle Sturtevant.

UNCLE STURTEVANT
Uh-oh. The human bean-sprout.

GODOT
Do not hurt others' feelings, Uncle Sturtevant. Yours are on the line, too.

UNCLE STURTEVANT
Oh. Well, Dottie, you are looking ravishing.

DOTTIE DUMPLING
I've been practicing.

UNCLE STURTEVANT
With Godot here?

DOTTIE DUMPLING
By myself.

UNCLE STURTEVANT
Very good policy. That's my method, too. But when one is ready for company -

DOTTIE DUMPLING
I am.

UNCLE STURTEVANT
I am, too.

(DOTTIE DUMPLING and UNCLE STURTEVANT kiss)

GODOT
I wonder if Cupid has taken up his cudgels.
(LUCILLE OUTBACK enters, saying)

LUCILLE OUTBACK
I have never heard of this Sappho; is she in the Social Register?

ALICE
(Following)
I think she antedates the Social Register. She owned an island off Greece called Lesbos.

LUCILLE OUTBACK
A big island?

ALICE
Huge.

LUCILLE OUTBACK
I would like to make her acquaintance.

ALICE
For the present, you'll have to settle for me.

LUCILLE OUTBACK
For what?

ALICE
For love.

LUCILLE OUTBACK
What love?

ALICE
My love.

LUCILLE OUTBACK
You love me? Where is Godot?

GODOT
Here, Lucille.

LUCILLE OUTBACK
What is this about love?

GODOT
What love?

LUCILLE OUTBACK
Alice has declared herself.

GODOT
Give her a kiss. That is the appropriate thing to do.

LUCILLE OUTBACK
But Mr. Godot, don't you see, she is a woman.

GODOT
Everyone knows that. And so are you.

LUCILLE OUTBACK
But I can't kiss a woman.

GODOT
Try.
(She tries, successfully)

ALICE
I have been practicing on Lady Daly.

LUCILLE OUTBACK
When the walls of Jericho fall, they crash.
(ALICE and LUCILLE OUTBACK kiss again)
(A and B enter)

A
Looks like the sexual revolution has finally taken off.

B
Taken off what?

A
You name it, here it is.

B
But what about Lady Daly?
(LADY DALY enters looking very forlorn)

LADY DALY
I've lost my horse.

A
Mare or stallion?

LADY DALY
Stallion. They give you the better ride.

B
Whatever happened to Dr. Habit?

LADY DALY
He's got a good seat.

GODOT
He hung himself. Over there.

LADY DALY
Is he dead yet?

GODOT
I forgot to look.

DANIEL
I'll take his pulse.
(DANIEL does so)

DANIEL
Cut him down, he's alive.
(Everyone gathers around HABIT, who comes to)

DR. LANCE HABIT
(Looking around)
I must be in Hell.

DANIEL
We are angels, you are not.

DOTTIE DUMPLING
We just saved you.

LADY DALY
For me.

DR. LANCE HABIT
God!

GODOT
Godot.

LADY DALY
Now it's my turn for a kiss.
(She administers one smack on HABIT's lips)
If you're going to be my husband, you're going to have to change your name. Your present cognomen does not apply.
(To everyone)
Any suggestions?
(Silence)

LADY DALY
(Continued)
Good. Then I choose – Lancelot Brown. You have the name, I am the number.
(She indicates the color of her skin)

BROWN
You're my wife?

LADY DALY
I'm the only one here who knows how to handle you.

BROWN
Oh, shit.

LADY DALY
You stop that right now. You don't know how lucky you are. You may be a doctor, but I am a patient, and that makes me your superior. Furthermore, we have abolished doctors here. They are superfluous, as everyone is well. If no one is sick, who needs welfare? Get up! Now it's my turn. Give me a kiss.

(BROWN does so)

LADY DALY
(Continued)
Honey, I'm going to call you Lord. Together we should do better than the Prince and Princess of Wales.

BROWN
I never thought I would conclude an interracial marriage.

GODOT
Many strange things are happening, all of them admirable.

BROWN
What would my mother say?

DOTTIE DUMPLING
I am sure she'd be pleased. Lady Daly is no dishrag. I would like to be a Lady, too.

GODOT
That can be arranged. Any other volunteers?

(Everyone volunteers)

GODOT
Before we all jump over the bridge, let me point out that privilege entails responsibility. How many of you want responsibility?

DANIEL
For what?

GODOT
Anything other than yourselves.

DOTTIE DUMPLING
I have trouble enough with myself.

LADY DALY
Me, too.
(All agree)

GODOT
Then I think titles would be inappropriate.

LADY DALY
Except for me.

GODOT
Lady Daly, your title is not a title, it is a name. Keep it well polished.

LADY DALY
Ok.

GODOT
Thank you. Dr. Habit, how do you feel? I mean Mr. Brown.

BROWN
About what?

GODOT
The state of the world.

BROWN
From here it looks distinctly more promising than previously.
(All agree)

GODOT
Could you tell me why?

BROWN
Because we love one another for what we are, not for what we are not.

GODOT
What comes next?
(BROWN is at a loss)

GODOT
(Continued)
Anybody?
(Silence)

DANIEL
We all love one another equally.

GODOT
You are brash for your age – and correct. Then?

DANIEL
Each one of us cleans up his mess.

DOTTIE DUMPLING
That's my line.

GODOT
It's correct. Thank you, both. So?
(Everybody goes about tidying up. The telephones are very busy as each inmate must account for a lot of bad past practices. Finally:)

GODOT
Are we ready?

DOTTIE DUMPLING
For what?

GODOT
This you must take on faith. Are we ready?
(All nod yes)

(There is a period of darkness, then light reappears on a cast outfitted each with a pair of wings)

GODOT
You are now raised to the rank of angels. Do not fall down. The world as you have known it is Hell, and no one who has known it and survived wants to repeat the experience. Am I right?

(All nod yes)

DOTTIE DUMPLING
What do we do now?

GODOT
Meet your neighbors. Anyone you pick will serve as your guide.

DOTTIE DUMPLING
Are we dead?

GODOT
My dear Dottie, now you are truly alive.

DANIEL
Can we ever go back?

GODOT
Do the right thing and you will never have to.

BROWN
Or want to. Purgatory is not pleasant.

DANIEL
Is the world still there?

GODOT
Forget the world. It has already forgotten you.

DANIEL
What do we do in Heaven?

GODOT
Whatever good you can imagine.

A
That will keep us busy for awhile.

GODOT
Imagination is infinite, so your business should last an eternity.

DANIEL
I think I'll go study infinitesimals.

DOTTIE DUMPLING
I shall dust.

LADY DALY
I'm going to work out.

A & B
We will do what we do best: wait for Godot.

GODOT
I shall keep you waiting.

DOTTIE DUMPLING
I shall preen my wings.

ALICE
I shall help you.

UNCLE STURTEVANT
I shall trust everyone.

BROWN
I shall become a patient. I need to relax.

LADY DALY
Darling.

DANIEL
The world is beginning to recede from sight.

      A
It is very beautiful.

      B
From a distance.

      A
I wonder if it will survive?

      B
Ask Godot.

      A
He's gone.

      B
He's gone back down.

      A
Someone must be waiting for him.

      B
Do they have time?

ACT III

SCENE 2

Patients' Garden.

    DANIEL
I think you are God.

    GODOT
God, Godot – what does a name mean?

    DANIEL
I don't know. I suppose a name has associations.

    GODOT
And mine?

    DANIEL
Godot means one thing, God another.

    GODOT
Am I allowed to choose my own name?

    DANIEL
Sure.

    GODOT
I'll stick with Godot.

    DANIEL
Isn't God more appropriate?

GODOT

Why?

DANIEL

Look at what's happening to the world!

GODOT

What?

DANIEL

It's becoming sane!

GODOT

(Laughing)

You are so amusing.

DANIEL

I'm serious.

GODOT

Don't rob me of my enjoyment of you, Daniel. You are right, the world in fact is getting its act together, with a little help.

DANIEL

You mean you.

GODOT

I mean everyone here.

DANIEL

The world is conquered by crazies!

GODOT

No. The Inmates of the Hospital hold a mirror up to the inhabitants of the world so that they may see.

DANIEL

See what?

GODOT

Themselves.

DANIEL
Oh. And you?

GODOT
I do my bit.
(DANIEL smiles)

DANIEL
I'll never catch you.

GODOT
One day I'll catch you, and then you'll have me.

DANIEL
I'm looking forward to it.

GODOT
You must earn what you are given. Even I have not yet finished with that.

DANIEL
No?

GODOT
I have not earned you.

DANIEL
But you have.

GODOT
That's what you think.

DANIEL
You don't see it?

GODOT
(Puzzled)
No.

DANIEL
Look around.

GODOT
(Looks around)
I don't see.

DANIEL
No. You are only used to seeing pain, primarily your own. To you, life is pain. And the rest is – well, not there.

GODOT
Good Heavens!
(He feels renewed - happiness is coming to him. He smiles broadly, then laughs)
This is something!

DANIEL
From now on, this is everything.

GODOT
How did you do that?

DANIEL
We are all - all - being elevated.

GODOT
To what?

DANIEL
Bliss.

GODOT
Good Heavens! What about the badness?

DANIEL
A Presidential pardon.

GODOT
Future standards of behavior?

DANIEL
Godot is here – somewhere. He is supposed to keep us in line, anonymously.

GODOT
You mean we are all equal - with one exception? And he moves amongst us just like anyone else?

DANIEL
You got it?

GODOT
Aren't I clever?

DANIEL
What?

GODOT
This was the only way I could assure equality and still avoid disputes. I hope it works. I am a god just like any other, except that I act as a preventative, unrecognizable as such. I hope you don't mind.

DANIEL
No.

GODOT
I hope no one else minds either. It was all I could do to come up with this solution. Otherwise we would have had the broils of Olympus on our hands.

DANIEL
Yes. Look!

(Enter LADY DALY and BROWN on skates)

LADY DALY
Whew! Lancelot, you are a whiz!

BROWN
I am learning fast.

LADY DALY
If you don't, you'll break a few bones.

BROWN
And my head, too.

LADY DALY
Oh, forget your head. You broke that a long time ago. It's irreparable; when we have some time we can get you a new one.

BROWN
I like the one I have.

LADY DALY
So do most people, but I hear that isn't going to get them very far.

BROWN
What do you mean?

LADY DALY
Ask Godot.

GODOT
(To BROWN)
Have a problem?

BROWN
Not any more.

DANIEL
I hope they're all that easy.

GODOT
Onwards!

DANIEL
Upwards!
(Enter ALICE and LUCILLE OUTBACK)
Now that I am no longer aristocratic, I am not afraid of change.

LUCILLE OUTBACK
What about yourself?

ALICE
Least of all in myself. That is what I can influence most directly.

LUCILLE OUTBACK
I love you more and more, and I don't even live on Lesbos.

ALICE
We can move.

LUCILLE OUTBACK
Do you suppose the whole world will change?

GODOT
It has the opportunity to do so.

ALICE
But what if some parts don't?

GODOT
Then we leave them behind.

LUCILLE OUTBACK
Here.

GODOT
Perhaps. Does it matter? The Universe is a big place. The Earth is of very recent vintage. It can be disposed of. Not even its closest neighbor will take notice.

DANIEL
God.

GODOT
Yes?

DANIEL
You mean?

GODOT
The Universe is many billions of years old. You are practically the most recent arrivals. You are therefore the most easily dispensed with. Don't worry, the good shall be preserved.

LUCILLE OUTBACK
What about the rest?

GODOT
Do you really want to know?

DANIEL
No.

ALICE
Yes!

GODOT
The wicked will be reduced to nothing. That is all.

LUCILLE OUTBACK
Aren't you being a little hard on the wicked?

GODOT
It is they who are hard, not I. In any event, they will soon have had all the chances they need.

DANIEL
How many is that?

GODOT
An infinite number. Study Newton's infinitesimal. I don't think anyone on earth has yet mastered it.

DANIEL
I have.

GODOT
Good for you.

LUCILLE OUTBACK
I don't want to be wicked anymore. What do I do?

GODOT
Alice will help you, and Dottie, and Uncle Sturtevant, and whoever else is around.

LUCILLE OUTBACK
How do I avoid the crowds?

ALICE
Don't give them an opening. If you do and you get fleeced, save the evidence and call the police.

DANIEL
The police will be working overtime.

GODOT
They already are. There is time. For overtime.

DANIEL
Oh.

(Enter DOTTIE and UNCLE STURTEVANT)

DOTTIE DUMPLING
Darling.

UNCLE STURTEVANT
Don't put on airs. We have company.

LUCILLE OUTBACK
Whose house is this, anyway?

UNCLE STURTEVANT
We have taken it over. It was abandoned.

LUCILLE OUTBACK
Well it isn't now. We all live here.

UNCLE STURTEVANT
Oh. Well, I have papers.

GODOT
Burn them. Or yourself. Take your pick.
(UNCLE STURTEVANT burns paper)

GODOT
You know what you are doing?
(UNCLE STURTEVANT shakes head no)

GODOT
You are saving yourself. Any questions?

UNCLE STURTEVANT
Who are you?
(GODOT looks to sky)

DANIEL
Another applicant to screen. What caliber mesh do you use, Herr Professor?

GODOT
Whatever suits the applicant. There are many beyond saving.

DANIEL
There are many who don't want to be saved.

GODOT
Same thing. It is hard work, saving yourself. Not everyone is up to it.

DANIEL
But they all have their chance.

GODOT
Many chances, many.

DANIEL
Have you set a deadline? It might be wise, or we may be waiting indefinitely.

GODOT
Yes. Next Wednesday.

DANIEL
Let's see. Today is Saturday – five days if you count at both ends.

GODOT
I do. So did the Romans.

DANIEL
Yes. Five days. And we're close to the end of the first.

GODOT
Don't worry, I put them all on notice last night.

DANIEL
All?

GODOT
Everyone. The dream you dream and remember is the important dream.

DANIEL
Will they dream it again?

GODOT
No. Some people don't know how to use their intention.

DANIEL
Attention.

GODOT
Both.

DANIEL
How do we go?

GODOT
That is my secret - for the present. I don't want to create a panic, and I am not interested in last-minute conversions. I am not a member of the Catholic Church.

DANIEL
What are you?

GODOT
I am myself, just as anyone else. All the rest is words founded on fear.

DANIEL
Fear?

GODOT
It was one of the devil's inventions. Very clever, death. Preceded by ignorance. And then all the rest. You know.

DANIEL
Yes. I do.

GODOT
I have done what I can. Now I wait - with you.

DANIEL
I love you.

GODOT
Many people say that. Few do it.

DANIEL
They have a little time.

GODOT
A little. What would you like to do with yours?

DANIEL
Play chess?

GODOT
I am not good at games. Do you think anyone will care?

DANIEL
About their own salvation? Of course.

GODOT
The evidence so far is not in your favor.
(DANIEL is silent)

DANIEL
Is there anything we can do?

GODOT
Take the good ones with us -

DANIEL
And leave the rest behind. What becomes of them?

GODOT
I have friends elsewhere. They are prepared to bring my career to its conclusion.

DANIEL
You?

GODOT
My career, not me.

DANIEL
Then?

GODOT
Then, as I have said, we shall all be equals before eternity.

DANIEL
And the wicked?

GODOT
They will have been reduced to nothing: along with their wickedness.

DANIEL
I can't wait.

GODOT
We can't be too hasty. We don't want any potential angels to slip us by.

DANIEL
We must be impeccable.

GODOT
Yes.

DANIEL
All the time.

GODOT
Yes.

DANIEL
And everyone else, too.

GODOT
Yes. And if you make mistakes - make them impeccably.

DANIEL
Yes. Mistakes are not wicked unless the intention behind them is wicked.

GODOT
Daniel, A and B have done their job well.

DANIEL
And me?

GODOT
And you, too. Shall we have something to eat?

DANIEL
We have only water.

GODOT
That will do.

DANIEL
Oh. I thought -

GODOT
Food is for pleasure. The body is very nearly all water. It is like

a battery, a water-battery full of electricity. All it needs most of the time is water.

DANIEL
I am not a biochemist.

GODOT
Neither am I.

DANIEL
Well, what would you like to do with your time?

GODOT
Make love.

DANIEL
But that is not allowed.

GODOT
By whom?

DANIEL
The Authorities.

GODOT
Who are they?

DANIEL
I don't know.

GODOT
Let us ignore them. They are of no account.

DANIEL
But they may kill you.

GODOT
They already have. Many times. And I am still here.

DANIEL
You are.

GODOT
The problem with previous inmates is that they allowed themselves to be killed. Catholicism is founded on cannibalism made into a cult. And the starting point is a murder. Can you imagine wearing a cross for life? It is lugubrious.

DANIEL
How did it get started?

GODOT
Don't ask me.

DANIEL
I won't. If we're not having dinner, what are we doing?

GODOT
Listening to the flowers.

DANIEL
Listening to the flowers? I thought one -

GODOT
Shh. Listen:
(He recites)
    I'd never seen them there before,
    It was as though the flowers were at war,
    The lungwort and the hellebore.
    But at closer sight,
    It was my mind that had put
    Each flower to flight,
    In fact, theirs was a dance
    Celebrating the marriage of a prince
    of Elms to a common maiden of the moss,
    A match that adumbrated no loss
    Of love on either side,
    Lacking impediment of pride,
    For love was the true metal
    That sent every petal

On its flight along the ground:
Love makes a sound
That even the deaf can hear,
So don't close up your ear,
The flowers are speaking to you very near.
I write in my spare time.

DANIEL
Oh, Mr. Godot, your poem is a treasure, and so are you.

GODOT
That's my job. Being a treasure.

DANIEL
Who gave it to you?

GODOT
I volunteered.

DANIEL
Volunteered?

GODOT
No one else wanted it.

DANIEL
Good Heavens!

GODOT
That's not what I would say. But it was my choice.

DANIEL
Couldn't you, well, tell what would happen?

GODOT
I suppose, but if I did, that would take all the air out of my tire. What would be the point? Unitary Omniscience? Perfect Protoplasm? I would rather be here with you, the flowers, my poem and -

DANIEL
A few clouds overhead.

GODOT
Soon enough they will go, and so will we.

DANIEL
What about the other Inmates?

GODOT
They are making the right choices. They have suffered enough, and so have we. Do you have faith in me?

DANIEL
Yes, yes.

GODOT
It is so hard to know sometimes, people do such strange and terrible things.

DANIEL
The devil -

GODOT
Yes, yes, the devil. He only provided the opportunity - the rest made their choices.

DANIEL
Why not continue -

GODOT
I am tired of the pain, and I think everyone else is, too. For those who aren't -

DANIEL
"The rest is silence."

GODOT
You got it.

DANIEL
Who wrote that?
(GODOT points to himself)

DANIEL
One more secret revealed.
(He laughs)
Where else have you been, my friend.

A
(To DANIEL)
You look very handsome.

DANIEL
It must be the weather.

GODOT
(To A)
Or you.

A
(To GODOT)
Or you.

GODOT
Soon enough we shall all have the powers of Proteus.

DOTTIE DUMPLING
Do you believe that?

UNCLE STURTEVANT
I think I need a few miracles to convince me.

GODOT
Back to the Catholics, eh? You need something to prop you up?

UNCLE STURTEVANT
Faith is a tricky thing.

DANIEL
Either you have it or you don't. Faith founded on miracles is not faith.

GODOT
Would you like a miracle?
(UNCLE STURTEVANT nods yes. GODOT nods and UNCLE STURTEVANT disappears in smoke)

DOTTIE DUMPLING
Where is he?

GODOT
He has been reduced to nothing.

DOTTIE DUMPLING
I don't believe you.
(She starts to cry)

GODOT
(About to nod again)
This is going to be a busy day.

DANIEL
Stop! Bring him back!

GODOT
Why? I am sure nothing is an improvement over this.
(He looks around)

DOTTIE DUMPLING
(Very sad)
He liked flowers. And your poem.

GODOT
Oh, well.
(UNCLE STURTEVANT reappears with some smoke and lightning)

UNCLE STURTEVANT
Why do you look like that?

GODOT
Miracles have that effect on some people.

UNCLE STURTEVANT
I don't believe in them.

GODOT
(To DOTTIE DUMPLING)
Here's your chance.
(DOTTIE DUMPLING is silent)

GODOT
Another time - I guess you don't love me as much now. And yet I shall bear full responsibility for what happens at the end.

DANIEL
Full responsibility?

GODOT
Yes, Daniel. It is part of who I am. I have already made my choices.

DANIEL
Can't you change?

GODOT
I can only go forwards, not backwards. The only way to go backwards is to start all over again, and that is something I definitely choose not to do. Things are arranged that way for you, too.

DANIEL
So we are all, everywhere, well acquainted with Hell.

GODOT
Yes.

DANIEL
And babies?

GODOT

Raw recruits, full of potential. I do not believe in Original Sin. Babies are not ready to make choices. When they begin, then their scales begin to weigh their souls.

DOTTIE DUMPLING

As it were.

GODOT

As it were.

UNCLE STURTEVANT

Am I sick again or are we being set up again for a fall?

GODOT

Neither. You are alive. Consider life the opportunity to improve yourself.

DOTTIE DUMPLING

In every way. See, Darling?

UNCLE STURTEVANT

Yes, yes, I see. But I like myself the way I am.

GODOT

Most people do. Otherwise they could not live with themselves. Now, why are you here?

UNCLE STURTEVANT

Because I could not live with myself.

GODOT

Now, do you want to change?

DANIEL

Oh, Uncle -

UNCLE STURTEVANT

Yes, I do. I do want to change. From my feet to my head. Ahh! There is so much to do!

GODOT
Daniel will help you. And Dottie, too.
(All three go to another part of the garden)

A
Monsieur Godot?

GODOT
Oui?

A
Now that we have finished waiting -

GODOT
But you haven't.

B
What!!

GODOT
The story is not over.

A
What's left?

GODOT
You want me to give it all away, FREE? The resu;ts would be dreadful, or, well, non-existent. I want something for me money, so you two wait - you'll get to the end with the rest of us.

A
Well, are we all going to die?

GODOT
Oh, well. You all are dead. That is why you are here. If you had been reduced to nothing, you would not be here. You would not be anywhere.

A
We're ghosts?

GODOT
That's about it.

A
And this is –

GODOT
Heaven – or part of it. The earth and heaven have amalgamated.

A
Where are the little devils?

B
Don't ask too many difficult questions.

GODOT
It's alright. The little devils were reduced to nothing.

B
When?

A
While we were talking. There must be a mess to clean up.

GODOT
There is always something for everyone to do.

B
Something for everyone.

A
I like that.

B
I think I love life – death, even ours.

A
Oh, B, now we are free! It didn't even hurt.

    B
I was not aware of it.

    GODOT
No. Only I.

    A
Thank you.

    B
Thank you.

    GODOT
You have yourselves to thank. You made the right choices.

    B
But you gave us choice.

    GODOT
Yes. Well. What else could I do? Create a puppet theater in which all the characters were mine?

    A
I don't think that would teach you much.

    B
We have learnt a lot from observation.

    GODOT
So have I.

    A
But –

    GODOT
What about the pain? As I have already said, I am a curious person, and I needed more knowledge than most.

    LADY DALY
Now Lancelot -

BROWN
Yes, my love.

LADY DALY
I feel different today. What's in those pills you give me?

BROWN
Nothing. They're placebos. Always were.

LADY DALY
What?

BROWN
Placebos. Sugar pills. Nothing. Though I do hear that some of your doctors prescribed poison for you.

LADY DALY
I'm dead.

BROWN
What!? You took them??

LADY DALY
Of course. So I must be dead.

GODOT
In Heaven we are all dead.

BROWN
We're in heaven?

LADY DALY
Looks that way. Here, you do the laundry today. I'm gonna go get a degree in psychology.

GODOT
Excuse me. Lady Daly - you already know more than most psychologists. Furthermore, they are now out of power, or should I say out of business.

LADY DALY
What can I do?

GODOT
Enjoy the flowers –

A
And the birds –

B
And the trees and ferns.

BROWN
And honeybees.

GODOT
Nature has much to teach us –

BROWN
Nature has much for us to enjoy.

GODOT
Find it, listen to it, it sings of all that is good in the world, even death, for death is always making room for rebirth and renewal.

LUCILLE OUTBACK
So I'm dead. Prove it.

ALICE
Shall I shoot you?

LUCILLE OUTBACK
Hah!
(ALICE pulls out a gun and shoots LUCILLE OUTBACK, who staggers a bit and then recovers her equilibrium)

LUCILLE OUTBACK
Missed!

ALICE
Right on target.

LUCILLE OUTBACK
My chest has a hole in it. You're right. Even if I wasn't dead, I am now. But what about you, Alice? Are you with me?

ALICE
I took an overdose last night. I'm deader than a duck.

LUCILLE OUTBACK
Trite but true. And the rest?

ALICE
They're all with us?

LUCILLE OUTBACK
Even Brown?

ALICE
Yes.

LUCILLE OUTBACK
He should change his name again.

ALICE
I suggest you keep your comments to yourself. Or you may end up downstairs.

(LUCILLE OUTBACK looks alarmed)

LUCILLE OUTBACK
Now that we are dead, what do we do with ourselves? Drink?

ALICE
That is one way to kill time.

LUCILLE OUTBACK
That is one way to kill yourself.

ALICE
It's slow, but it works.

LUCILLE OUTBACK
Great way to fool yourself into thinking you still are alive.

ALICE
Yes. How are you doing? Now that I'm dead, I don't find alcohol necessary or attractive. It tastes terrible.

LUCILLE OUTBACK
Yes. I've given it up.

ALICE
What about all those parties?

LUCILLE OUTBACK
Pure emptiness.

ALICE
You are not empty.

LUCILLE OUTBACK
Nor you.

ALICE
Do you like it here?

LUCILLE OUTBACK
Yes.

ALICE
Shall we stay?

LUCILLE OUTBACK
Let's.

ALICE
Any application to fill out?

LUCILLE OUTBACK
No one's thrown us out.

ALICE
True.

LUCILLE OUTBACK
Let's stay.

ALICE
Yes.

BROWN
I cannot bloody understand it. Every time I prick your finger, I get no blood.

LADY DALY
We have already had our bloodletting. And there is no more blood left.

BROWN
But you need blood to be alive.

LADY DALY
The obvious conclusion -

BROWN
(Screams)
You're dead!

LADY DALY
(Laughs)
Hey, honey, don't get too agitated or you'll need a placebo to calm you down. Anyway, I hate the sight of blood, especially my own. It makes me faint.
(Suddenly there is a bright light shining on a spot on stage. GODOT walks into the spot and disappears)

LUCILLE OUTBACK
Where's he gone?

DANIEL
To find a few fresh souls to translate up here.

LADY DALY
Up here?
(Stage is engulfed in clouds)

DOTTIE DUMPLING
Looks like we really are on high.

LADY DALY
Or high on high.

DANIEL
Just high.
(The clouds consume everyone)

-FINIS-

Godot, Alive or Dead

A Drama

CAST OF CHARACTERS

GODOT

LADY DALY: a large black woman in her early thirties, manic-depressive with aggressive tendencies

DOTTIE DUMPLING: A maid, thin

UNCLE STURTEVANT: A Southerner suffering from megalomania

DANIEL: Black-haired twenty-two-year-old, very handsome

ALICE: Waitress (former Princess)

LUCILLE: A Society Person

MR. MALAPROP: A loose tongue

LANCELOT BROWN: Former Resident-in-Chief of Westchester Clinic, attached to Lady Daly

POPE

CARDINAL

CANDY/SHEPHERD

PERDITA/SHEPHERD (Candy's sister)

ACT I

SCENE 1

First, a mental hospital in Westchester County, as in Godot Imagine Godot. Afterwards, a barren waste in the Outer Hebrides, as in Godot Arrives.

    GODOT
I think I've used up everything, including myself.

    LADY DALY
Nonsense. You're depressed.

    GODOT
But we are free.

    LADY DALY
That's why we are all depressed.

    GODOT
I guess life is not such a great gift, after all.

    LADY DALY
It depends whose life you are talking about.

    DOTTIE DUMPLING
I like to clean.

    GODOT
That's my job. I'm the responsible party.

UNCLE STURTEVANT
We are all the responsible party.

DOTTIE DUMPLING
Look at me!
(They all look)

DANIEL
Even I am responsible, and I'm still an adolescent.

GODOT
You're precocious.

DANIEL
So are you.

GODOT
(Laughs)
Every time I drop trou, someone notices.

DANIEL
We are only trying to help.

LADY DALY
Yes.

ALICE
We do love you.

GODOT
Love, love.

ALICE
Is it such a bad thing?

GODOT
It seems to excuse a lot of things.

DOTTIE
We love you without excuse.

DANIEL
Mr. Godot, Dottie and the rest of us are quite sincere.

GODOT
What of all the rest we have left behind?

LADY DALY
They have earned their fate.

ALICE
And we have earned ours.

LUCILLE
And what is that?

GODOT
Perpetual happiness? I am only guessing.
(Pause)
Think about it.
(They think)

GODOT
Is that really what you want? Eternity? Happiness?
(They all think some more)

UNCLE STURTEVANT
Well, at least we are not crazy any more.

DOTTIE
You can appreciate my labors.

GODOT
You can all appreciate your own.

ALICE
The sunset is nice.

DANIEL
Girls are sometimes beautiful.

GODOT
You can be beautiful.

LADY DALY
We can all be beautiful.

LUCILLE
That is true.

GODOT
But the rest?

DANIEL
The living?

GODOT
Yes.

DANIEL
They are falling into eternity, and they have no idea where it will take them.

LADY DALY
Where?

GODOT
I can no longer see into the future.

DANIEL
That is because you are dead, too. You have assumed your mortality. And here is where you end up.

DOTTIE
But where are we?

LUCILLE
With each other.

DOTTIE
But where?

GODOT
At am asylum, some 30 minutes by a short drive north of New York City.

LUCILLE
Something is becoming clear.
(They all look at LUCILLE)

LUCILLE
Life had its purpose. Death does, too. Like life, it has the purpose we give to it.

DOTTIE
You see!

GODOT
What about happiness? What about eternity?

UNCLE STURTEVANT
Straw dogs. Just like me. I used to think I was everything. Now I know I am nothing.

DANIEL
And the rest of us.
(To GODOT)
You have made your choices. You are still free to make more. We are all free to make more.
(Light begins to dim)

LADY DALY
The sun is setting.

GODOT
It is time to act.
(They all look at GODOT)

DANIEL
Action is dear.

LADY DALY
Words are not.

DOTTIE
Are we moving?

GODOT
You will see.
(Slow fade to BLACKOUT)

ACT I

SCENE 2

        DANIEL
There is no way out of here.

        GODOT
We are all free to leave.

        DANIEL
What about the living?

        DOTTIE
We can haunt them.

        LUCILLE
We already do.

        LADY DALY
Where are they?

        DANIEL
Outside.

        LADY DALY
Outside what?

        DANIEL
Outside us.

UNCLE STURTEVANT
This is getting us nowhere.

MR. MALAPROP
This is where we are.

GODOT
One puzzle after another.

ALICE
Maybe we should stop thinking.

LADY DALY
Maybe we should do something.
(Pause)

DOTTIE
Time is passing.
(She dusts)

GODOT
I suppose I should help clean.

UNCLE STURTEVANT
Haven't we been here before?

DANIEL
Where?

UNCLE STURTEVANT
Immobilized.

GODOT
What?

UNCLE STURTEVANT
By anguish.

DANIEL
Godot was in anguish. Don't you remember how he writhed on the floor?

(All nod)

DANIEL
(Continuing)
He set us free.

GODOT
You have always been free.

DOTTIE
I need to move, constantly.

LUCILLE
I enjoy watching the weather.

UNCLE STURTEVANT
It seems to move.

LUCILLE
What can move us?

ALICE
A little genealogy.

UNCLE STURTEVANT
Presumption.

DANIEL
Sex.

LUCILLE
Alcohol.

LADY DALY
Food.

DOTTIE
The four food groups.

LADY DALY
Alcohol, caffeine, fat, and sugar. I love them all.

GODOT
(Pauses)
Which way are we going now?

DOTTIE
The dust is not very heavy today.

GODOT
You needn't collect it, my dear.

DOTTIE
Well...

DANIEL
Is there love in youth?

GODOT
I never had a youth.

LUCILLE
And old age?

GODOT
Do I look old?

LADY DALY
Does anyone here look old, now that we are dead?

DANIEL
We are subjects of arrested development.

UNCLE STURTEVANT
I was once arrested, for threatening suicide.

DANIEL
Really?

UNCLE STURTEVANT
They locked me up in a hospital, not like this one. For three days. As a precaution. And they gave me pills. They made me sleep. When I woke up...

DANIEL
Back to suicide?

UNCLE STURTEVANT
That is the story of my life.

LUCILLE
And mine. Alcohol is a slow way to go.

DOTTIE
If you dust, you die only at a great age. My grandmother was 95 when she went, and she had dusted for ages.

GODOT
The common lot.

DANIEL
Where do I fit in? I don't dust, and I have never contemplated killing myself.

UNCLE STURTEVANT
You will.

LUCILLE
Then you will be an adult. Welcome to the club.

DANIEL
I don't think I want to grow up – at least not any further.

GODOT
You won't.

LADY DALY
You are already dead at an early age. Now the only thing to do is make peace with yourself.

DANIEL
You are very philosophical.

LADY DALY
Kid, with my experience, either you learn or you die.

LUCILLE
Or both.

UNCLE STURTEVANT
I think we are doing all just fine.

DOTTIE
We are keeping each other company.

ALICE
The conversation is interesting.

GODOT
There are no authorities.

LUCILLE
I feel a little faded.

MR. MALAPROP
Comme ci, comme ça. Or, as it were.

GODOT
I must stretch my legs.

LADY DALY
I must stretch my mind.
(LADY DALY looks at the audience)

DOTTIE
I must stretch the dust, or I shall have nothing to do for eternity.

LUCILLE
I must stretch my drink.

UNCLE STURTEVANT
I am going to stretch my power.

DANIEL
And I, my love.

GODOT
I shall stretch time, all of it.

DANIEL
I am learning about string theory.

GODOT
That will help.

ALICE
I want to stretch myself.
(There is perfect silence)

MR. MALAPROP
The truth seems to be elastic, strings or no strings.

UNCLE STURTEVANT
I can pull strings.

LADY DALY
Is that why you are here?
(There is silence)

LUCILLE
I experience oblivion every night.

LADY DALY
Lady, you sure do get your exercise.

ALICE
I am afraid of my inferiors.

DOTTIE
I will put salt in your coffee.

DANIEL
I need technical sex training.

GODOT
At your service.

DANIEL
You! Again! I thought we broke up in the interregnum.

GODOT
That was just a rest period between bouts of intellectual and emotional creativity.

LADY DALY
I'll create you, if you don't watch out.

GODOT
I think I shall go back to being alone.

UNCLE STURTEVANT
So that's where you come from!

DANIEL
Now we know.

GODOT
You do not know where I come from. You cannot guess what preceded my solitude.

(They are all stumped)

DOTTIE
A little rag?

GODOT
Practically.

LADY DALY
Nothing!

GODOT
Now we revert to what we know.

LADY DALY
And we cannot know nothing because nothing does not exist!

GODOT
Lady Daly, you are the crown jewel of humankind. I love you.

DANIEL
We all love you.
(GODOT looks slighted)
DANIEL
(To GODOT)
I think you may be an imposter.

LANCELOT BROWN
Here I am!

LADY DALY
I thought you had rejoined the living.

BROWN
We were divorced, but I still love you.

LADY DALY
Ready for Round Two?

BROWN
Now that we are no longer married, we can enjoy ourselves.

LADY DALY
Promiscuous!

BROWN
Psychotherapists of all conditions prescribe love as the best cure-all.

GODOT
What is love?

ALICE
Where are we going?

LUCILLE
It's alright, dear. I was really only interested in your real estate.

MR. MALAPROP
I resign.

DOTTIE
From what?

MR. MALAPROP
My position as Sibyl.

LADY DALY
How many positions did she have?

MR. MALAPROP
It is easier to be a stenographer.

GODOT
I can see we are re-casting ourselves in a new light.

ALICE
What?

LUCILLE
What?

GODOT
Even though we are dead, we are subject to change.

DOTTIE
I want to be myself, permanently.

LADY DALY
I don't ever want to be myself again.

MR. MALAPROP
Slower, please, I am trying to take notes.

GODOT
Don't. They won't be of any use; where are we going, the uses of history are extinct.

DANIEL
But we are extinct.

GODOT
That is what I have been saying all along.

MR. MALAPROP
Where is A? He has missed the whole show!

LUCILLE
A no-show.

DANIEL
I'll show him.

MR. MALAPROP
What?

DANIEL
What, what?

MR. MALAPROP
(Patiently)
What will you show him?

DANIEL
We can all change.

ALICE
Especially in his absence.

DANIEL
Godot has been absent for a long time.

UNCLE STURTEVANT
And now that he is here?

DANIEL
He is still a no-show.

GODOT
Which is why you are all free.

LADY DALY
Thank God!

GODOT
Thank me.

ACT I

SCENE 3

        DANIEL
I just want to write.

        GODOT
Write what?

        DANIEL
An autobiography.

        GODOT
But you're only twenty.

        DANIEL
Twenty-two.

        GODOT
Even better.

        DANIEL
Two years can make all the difference.

        GODOT
Do I make a difference?

        DANIEL
Yes.
(GODOT and DANIEL kiss)

DANIEL
Now, you'll never go back to women.

GODOT
You are handsome.

DANIEL
Really?

GODOT
I am known for my good taste.
(They kiss)

DANIEL
Delicious.

GODOT
How far do you want to go?

DANIEL
Just a kiss. For now.

GODOT
You tantalize me.

DANIEL
I am still a virgin.

GODOT
I am not.

DANIEL
Ah, well.

GODOT
Do you love me?

DANIEL
Sometimes.

GODOT
You continue to tantalize me.

DANIEL
I want you to build up some steam.

GODOT
Something is building up.
(GODOT puts his hands between his legs)

DANIEL
Here. Some grated potato, egg, milk, onion, and a frying pan with some oil.

GODOT
Where's the oil?

DANIEL
Here.

GODOT
Oh.

DANIEL
There is nothing like one of Aunt Gertrude's potato pancakes with applesauce.

GODOT
I like French.

DANIEL
French what?

GODOT
Food.

DANIEL
This is more substantial.

GODOT
Good God!

DANIEL
These are just the preliminaries.

GODOT
I hope so. Are you sure you don't want to go out? French cuisine is the highest of them all, except, perhaps, for the Chinese.

DANIEL
They will eat anything.

GODOT
So will I.

DANIEL
Behave!

GODOT
I am trying.

DANIEL
It isn't every day that I prepare dinner.

GODOT
It isn't every day that I offer myself to someone.

DANIEL
It can wait. You yourself said we have eternity in front of us.

GODOT
We do.
(GODOT looks auguished)

DANIEL
In that case, we have time for potato pancakes.

GODOT
I rather like French food.

DANIEL
I am sorry. Anyway, you are repeating yourself.

GODOT
I'll try not to. But with so much time to pass…

DANIEL
Things could get a little dreary. Even love.

GODOT
Yes.

DANIEL
Has this happened to you before?

GODOT
You have no idea.

DANIEL
I can imagine.

GODOT
Life is too short.

DANIEL
Death is beginning to look too long.

GODOT
That is why I clean out the memory every so often. Then I can repeat myself without knowing it.

DANIEL
What?

GODOT
If I have to face eternity, I'd like to do it with you.

DANIEL
The pancakes are almost done.

GODOT
So am I.
(GODOT puts a hand on DANIEL'S thigh)

DANIEL
Oh....
(BLACKOUT)

ACT II

SCENE 1

Enter all the actors from Act I dressed in black academic gowns, except for GODOT, who is dressed in white priest's vestments and DANIEL, in combat fatigues.
Stage Right – a throne. Throne is occupied by the POPE, who is dressed as a clown.

    POPE
Sit down.
(They all sit)
    POPE
(To GODOT)
Who are you?
    GODOT
Don't you know?
    POPE
I ask, you respond. Who are you?
    GODOT
I am Godot.
    POPE
And who is Godot?
(GODOT is silent)

POPE
(Continuing)
Does anyone here know this soul?
(There is silence)

POPE
(Continuing)
Speak up. Does anyone know who this man is?

DOTTIE
He helps me clean.

UNCLE STURTEVANT
He has fixed my brain – and my family relations.

LADY DALY
We're pals from way back.

LANCE
He has brought me down to earth.
(POPE raises eyeglasses)

LANCE
(Continuing)
Well, when we were alive, he brought me down.

POPE
Anyone else?

ALICE
He has given me a job which I enjoy.

POPE
(To ALICE)
You look familiar.

ALICE
Your Honor, we have had several audiences together.

POPE
Yes. You are a Princess.

ALICE
I was a Princess. Now I am a waitress at the Hard Luck Café, here in Heaven.

POPE
Yes. I think you have waited on me.

LADY DALY
We have been waiting on you for a long time.
(The POPE ignores LADY DALY)

DOTTIE
(Hopefully)
We enjoy our work.

LUCILLE
I am a socialite, and I can vouch for Godot. His lineage is spectacular.

POPE
Thank you. Anyone else?

DANIEL
We are lovers.
(The POPE looks interested)

DANIEL
We are monogamous.
(The POPE shrugs)

DANIEL
We have been waiting for Mr. Godot for a very long time, and now he is here.

UNCLE STURTEVANT
He is not what we were expecting.

DOTTIE & OTHERS
No. Not at all.

POPE
What were you expecting?

DOTTIE
Well, something like you. A little flashy, with some music, background lights, massive architecture, and an aquiline nose.

POPE
Nose?

DOTTIE
You do look aquiline to me.

LUCILLE
To me, too. Very distinguished.

POPE
Thank you. But you are not here to flatter me.

LADY DALY
We were wondering, now that we are in Heaven, if you could judge us. Sort of set your seal of approval on us. Make us feel at home.

DOTTIE
And secure.

GODOT
You see –

POPE
Not you.
(To DOTTIE)
Continue.

DOTTIE
We don't want to go back.

LADY DALY
And we need to know who Godot is, or was, or –

POPE
What makes you think this is Heaven?

DOTTIE
There are no trees.

LUCILLE
Or grass.

UNCLE STURTEVANT
Or flowers.

GODOT
Rather like the Outer Hebrides.
(The POPE nods)

GODOT
(Continuing)
O!

DANIEL
There are lots of clouds.

LUCILLE
It is just as I had imagined it.

DOTTIE
Yes. And it is not dirty.
(DOTTIE looks a little despondent)

DOTTIE
(Continuing)
What am I going to do?

POPE
But what makes you think this is Heaven?

LUCILLE
No cocktails, not even any family trees.

LADY DALY
I don't see too many Black people here.

POPE
Most of them are in Heaven.

LADY DALY
If they are in Heaven, where are we?

GODOT
The Outer Hebrides.

(At this point, a SHEPHERD BOY appears, dressed in a kilt)

GODOT
Oh, someone young.

DANIEL
Competition.

POPE
Quiet!
(To the SHEPHERD)
Do you know where you are?

SHEPHERD
I am lost.

POPE
Where do you come from?

SHEPHERD
My village.

POPE
And where is that?

SHEPHERD
In the Outer Hebrides.

GODOT
I told you so.

POPE
Are you looking for something?

SHEPHERD
I have lost my sheep. I fell asleep – I am all alone – sometimes I must sleep – and they wandered off. If my master finds out.

DOTTIE
We can help you look for them.

UNCLE STURTEVANT
Of course.
(The others agree)

GODOT
Can you point us in the right direction?

SHEPHERD
I don't know.
(SHEPHERD begins to cry)

GODOT
It's all right.
(The others begin to see that the SHEPHERD, besides being young, is also very beautiful)

LUCILLE
Well, dearie, would you like me to make you some lemonade?
(SHEPHERD nods no)
(LUCILLE makes some anyway)

LUCILLE
Here. It will take your mind off your troubles.

DOTTIE
Let me clean your shoes.

(DOTTIE takes them off and begins to clean them)

LADY DALY

Do you like music? I was in a Brooklyn choir. Baptist. Very high church.

(SHEPHERD doesn't know what to say)
(LADY DALY sings a hymn)

LANCELOT

I didn't know you could sing.

POPE

Stop!

(LADY DALY stops)

POPE

This is not a circus.

(Everyone begins to laugh – as the POPE is dressed as a clown)

POPE

Stop! Stop!

(They all laugh louder)
(The POPE begins to smile. Then he laughs, too)

GODOT

Make I speak now?

(POPE keeps laughing)

GODOT

It seems we have returned to Earth.

(Everyone stops laughing. POPE exits)

LADY DALY

No joke?

GODOT

No joke.

DOTTIE

Why?

LUCILLE
Anyone can see why. To help the Shepherd, of course.

UNCLE STURTEVANT
What about the Pope?

(Everyone suddenly notices the POPE has disappeared)

DANIEL
Some joke.

ALICE
But where is he?

GODOT
I have sent him back up into The Clouds.

UNCLE STURTEVANT
Uh – oh.

GODOT
Purgatory.

LADY DALY
Were we ever in Heaven?

ALICE
I was once a Princess, and it was not Heaven.

UNCLE STURTEVANT
I was once Emperor of the Universe, and it was Hell.

DOTTIE
There is no garbage in Heaven.

SHEPHERD
(Hopefully)
There is no garbage here.

GODOT
Right.

ALICE
Then this is Heaven?

GODOT
This is the Outer Hebrides. For the time being, you are in Heaven.

LADY DALY
You mean –

GODOT
Yes, Lady Daly. Heaven is a state of mind, not body, and you are all in it.

SHEPHERD
And me?

GODOT
You are a treasure whom all of us respect.

DOTTIE
I loved him at first sight.

GODOT
So did we all.

SHEPHERD
Can I go now?

DOTTIE
But we want you to stay.

SHEPHERD
But my sheep –

ALICE
They are lost.

GODOT
Yes.

SHEPHERD
I must find them.

ALICE
May we help?

GODOT
Of course. That is why we are here.
(Everyone begins to smile a lot. They point to each other's heads as if to say "Heaven")

LANCELOT
This is the price we pay for our sins.

UNCLE STURTEVANT
Sins?

LADY DALY
I know about sinful, and we aren't it.

GODOT
Yes.

LADY DALY
We are sick.

DOTTIE
And now we are well.
(The SHEPHERD leads them all offstage)

ACT II

SCENE 2

DANIEL
(By himself)
I wonder where they have all gone...
(He wanders around stage absent-mindedly, then sits on a rock)

DANIEL
I could sing.
(He tries a hymn)

DANIEL
Ugh.
(He tries a Broadway show tune)

DANIEL
Solitude is confinement.
(He gets up and resumes wandering)

DANIEL
I hope I don't spend eternity alone, here.
(There is a crack of thunder)

DANIEL
I think salvation is near.
(The POPE appears, dressed in Papal vestments)

POPE
Greetings.

DANIEL
Hello.

POPE
Where is everyone?

DANIEL
I think they're resting.

POPE
Good idea.
(The POPE smiles widely. Daniel looks alarmed)

POPE
And you, dearie, how old are you?

DANIEL
Thirty-nine.

POPE
You can't be more than an adolescent.
(DANIEL does not respond)

POPE
You are very handsome.
(Pauses)
Was that your father with you?
(The POPE imitates GODOT in a gesture)

DANIEL
We are just friends.

POPE
You said you were lovers.

DANIEL
It's platonic.

POPE
I am not a follower of Plato. In fact, I have never read him. He is a bit too much of an Idealist. Long-winded, too. I prefer Heracleitus, or, maybe Parmenides.

DANIEL
Or maybe –

POPE
(Cutting him off)
You are a student somewhere?

DANIEL
I have no home, and I only have myself to study.

POPE
What about Godot?

DANIEL
He is only a friend.

POPE
(Thinking he is getting somewhere)
Do you have any other friends?

DANIEL
Just the ones you have seen.

POPE
But they are all old.

DANIEL
You are no youth yourself.

POPE
I am the Pope!

DANIEL
What are you doing here?
(The POPE ignores this)

DANIEL
(Continuing)
If you are here, you must be dead.

POPE
Pooh. If I were dead, I would not be here, with you. I would be in Heaven.

DANIEL
Or somewhere else.

POPE
(Getting a little agitated)
Look here, I'm the Pope and you are very attractive. Wouldn't you like to get to know me better?

DANIEL
I think I'd rather not know you at all.
(The POPE attempts an embrace)

DANIEL
Get out of here!

POPE
So young and so untender.

DANIEL
I'm leaving.
(DANIEL stays. GODOT enters)

GODOT
Very heroic.

POPE
What?

GODOT
I say your love making is very heroic, but it won't do. It just won't wash at all.

POPE
Wash what?

GODOT
Your soul?

POPE
I am an expert on souls, and you are no one.

GODOT
Yes. Well, I don't see much point in your making passes at young men. You are old, and you have never in your life been very attractive.

POPE
I am the Pope, and I can have what I want.

GODOT
I am Godot, and I think you are making a bad mistake.

POPE
(Indicating DANIEL)
I think it is up to the young man to decided between us.

DANIEL
(To the POPE)
You're just a clown.

GODOT
(Smiling)
In fact, you are dead, and your soul, and a few others, need to be retro-fitted.

POPE
I am quite aware of my soul. And I am not dead. And if anyone here needs a soul, it is you.
(To DANIEL)
And you, too. You should take pity on an old man who has everyone's best interests at heart all the time, except for his own. I didn't want to be Pope. I was chosen – or elected. When

I was a Cardinal, I could do what I wanted. Now, I have to put up with nonsense all the time. It is not fair. I'm supposed to pray half the day, and spend the rest of the time looking after a lot of people just as sinful as I am. I want freedom. But I am Pope and I have nothing, nothing for myself at all.

DANIEL
You have us, if you like.

POPE
How, how can you say that? You both have just rejected me. And you say I am dead. If I am dead, how can I be here with you?
(Alarmed)
Where are we anyway?

GODOT
In the Outer Hebrides.

POPE
I have never heard of them.

DANIEL
I'll draw you a map.
(DANIEL draws on the ground)

DANIEL
(Continuing)
Rome is here, all of Italy here, France next, then the Channel and England, and then Scotland and the Outer Hebrides.

POPE
I am afraid.

GODOT
You needn't be. You are Pope.

POPE
But I have just exposed myself completely.

GODOT
Yes, and it doesn't matter.

POPE
You mean I can do whatever I want?

GODOT
I don't think that is the conclusion I would draw. But, yes, you are free to do what you want.

DANIEL
What do you choose to do?

GODOT
(After a pause)
We are here, waiting.

DANIEL
Here we are.

POPE
O, can't you just leave me alone? O, that is your line.
(DANIEL laughs. GODOT looks pleased)

POPE
O, I am even more afraid of you now. How can I do the right thing? O, I am so compromised!

GODOT
Not at all. You are dead. And you can do whatever you like. Just like life.

POPE
But I told you when I was Pope, but I still am Pope, or perhaps – am I really dead?

GODOT
I see a big "D" on your forehead.

DANIEL
Today is Ash Wednesday.

POPE
And I am dead.

(Big pause)
Well, I guess running after Daniel isn't my prime object in life – in death.

DANIEL
You will find many more like me if you stick around.

POPE
I am sticking.

GODOT
I suggest you take a tour of the premises for a while, and then come back and tell us what you think. You may change your state of mind.

DANIEL
That is what I did.

GODOT
Yes. Then you can approach us both from the right point of view. Love need not be ugly.

(GODOT and DANIEL exit together. POPE falls to the ground and begins to cry and tries to pray, but he can not pray)

ACT II

SCENE 3

GODOT
I was just trying to remind him of what he already knows.

LUCILLE
That is what we all already know.

ALICE
I think we forgot it.

UNCLE STURTEVANT
Somewhere.

ALICE
Maybe in childhood.

DANIEL
Or later.

GODOT
Maybe. Maybe some people never forget.

DANIEL
And some people never remember.
(POPE enters)

POPE
O, my brain. I am in such pain!

LUCILLE
I guess if Heaven is in the head, so is Purgatory.
(GODOT smiles)

ALICE
You know, Mr. Godot, we all love you.

GODOT
I believe it.

LUCILLE
Your blessings were definitely not what we were expecting.

UNCLE STURTEVANT
(Somewhat dubious)
Is there more to come?
(GODOT smiles but says nothing)

GODOT
There is always more to come, otherwise you would not be dead. Life is very limited.
(SHEPHERD enters)

DANIEL
What are you doing here?

SHEPHERD
I found one sheep.
(He pulls on a chain he had been carrying that extends off stage. A CARDINAL enters. Everyone is transfixed)

GODOT
Where have you been looking?

LUCILLE
Rome?

ALICE
Boston?

GODOT
Anywhere else?

DANIEL
Take your pick.

DOTTIE
Do I have a clean-up job ahead of me, or what?

GODOT
I must go buy a blackboard.
(GODOT exits)

DANIEL
Uh oh.

ALICE
Now we get a lecture, and I always hated my lessons.

LUCILLE
I had a few lessons.

UNCLE STURTEVANT
And now we are here.

LADY DALY
You said it.

SHEPHERD
Now, I am here.

DANIEL
You must be dead.

SHEPHERD
Me? Dead? I don't believe it.

CARDINAL
(Moaning)
Someone has caught me.

DANIEL
What?

CARDINAL
Someone caught me *in flagrante delicto.*

LUCILLE
With this Shepherd?

CARDINAL
Yes.

ALICE
How did you die?

CARDINAL
The starving masses strung us up.

SHEPHERD
(Offering)
In plain sight of the sky.

CARDINAL
I am guilty of so much.

LUCILLE
Have you ever been out of your mind?

CARDINAL
No.

ALICE
Now that you are dead –

CARDINAL
I do feel somewhat odd. Very peculiar.

DANIEL
He's out of it.

UNCLE STURTEVANT
Let him suffer for a while.

LUCILLE
We'll bring you along in good time.

CARDINAL
Time, time, I had a good time, until now.

LUCILLE
Do you know where you are?
(CARDINAL shakes his head)

DANIEL
In the Outer Hebrides.

CARDINAL
Dead and in the Outer Hebrides?

UNCLE STURTEVANT
There is no one here but us.

DANIEL
And Mr. Godot.

LUCILLE
And the Pope.

CARDINAL
(Alarmed)
Oh. Oh, no.

ALICE
What's the matter?

CARDINAL
Are you sure I'm dead?

ALICE
Yes.

CARDINAL
May I confess?

ALICE
It might make you feel better.

UNCLE STURTEVANT
You may face Purgatory.

DANIEL
Or beyond.

CARDINAL
Beyond?

DANIEL
Heaven is beyond Purgatory.

CARDINAL
We killed the Pope.

EVERYONE
What?!

CARDINAL
There was a cabal against him, and we killed him.
(Everyone is dumbfounded)

LUCILE
What on earth?

CARDINAL
I know, I know. Well, even the new millennium can contain a few old jokes.

DANIEL
Jokes?

CARDINAL
I was to replace him.

DANIEL
As Pope?
(The CARDINAL nods)

DANIEL
Oh.
(SHEPHERD begins to cry)

DANIEL
(Pointing to the SHEPHERD)
What about him?

CARDINAL
He was my catamite.

DANIEL
I thought he was a Shepherd, looking for his sheep.

SHEPHERD
I went astray.

CARDINAL
He just wandered in one day, and I took him.

SHEPHERD
I tried to resist.

CARDINAL
It was only a one-night stand.

SHEPHERD
It hurt.

DANIEL
I am sure it did. Look here.
(To the CARDINAL)
Do you think you might do this boy a penance?

CARDINAL
Anything.

DANIEL
Help him find his sheep.
(SHEPHERD and CARDINAL exit)

LUCILLE
Where's Papa?

UNCLE STURTEVANT
The Pope is exploring the Hinterlands.

ALICE
I saw him a while ago North-Northwest of here.

DANIEL
Shall I go find him?

LUCILLE
Let him find us. There is not much out there, and we are here, and he will come back.

DANIEL
What if he meets the Cardinal?

LUCILLE
Such is the difficulty of death: sooner or later you meet up with every one of the people you don't want to see.

DANIEL
Slaves.

UNCLE STURTEVANT
Victims.

LUCILLE
The ugly.

ALICE
The powerful.

UNCLE STURTEVANT
The crazies we wronged.

LUCILLE
The crazies we were.

DANIEL
We have already examined ourselves.

LUCILLE
And our histories.

UNCLE STURTEVANT
Our past.

LUCILLE
Now we are better.

UNCLE STURTEVANT
Now we are better off.

LUCILLE
I suppose.

DANIEL
What about the Pope and the Cardinal?

LUCILLE
Sooner or later we'll get them together –

DANIEL
And see what happens.

LUCILLE
Yes.

UNCLE STURTEVANT
Yes.

ALICE
Yes.

DANIEL
Yes.

ACT II

SCENE 4

Another part of the Outer Hebrides.

POPE
This looks familiar.
(The POPE gazes into the audience. Then he turns to upstage right and left)
POPE
Where am I?
(SHEPHERD appears)
SHEPHERD
Sir?
POPE
Child?
SHEPHERD
I am lost.
POPE
I am, too.
SHEPHERD
I was abused.

POPE
I was, too. Now we are free, to be ourselves.

SHEPHERD
But I am not grown-up. How can I ever realize myself? How can I grow up, now that I am dead?

POPE
(Crying)
The things we do to satisfy ourselves.

SHEPHERD
Are you my master?

POPE
Master? Here?

SHEPHERD
There is no one else.

POPE
I suppose I can volunteer.

SHEPHERD
I cannot find my master, nor my sheep – except one.

POPE
One?

SHEPHERD
Yes, one. He was dressed all in red.

POPE
Red?

SHEPHERD
Yes.

POPE
Did he have horns?

SHEPHERD
I don't know.

POPE
A tail?

SHEPHERD
Maybe. But I didn't really notice. I don't know. I am only a boy.

POPE
It must have been the Devil. Or the Anti-Christ.

SHEPHERD
Who are they?

POPE
(Ignoring him)
I knew I would have to deal with him sooner or later.

SHEPHERD
Sooner or later?

POPE
Yes.

SHEPHERD
I am afraid.

POPE
Don't be afraid. Please. I'll help you. But you must help me find him. He is very dangerous.

SHEPHERD
I have a rope.
(SHEPHERD produces the rope)

POPE
Good. Let's see if we can track him down.
(They wander off)

ACT III

SCENE 1

The POPE enters with SHEPHERD GIRL.

GIRL
Where did he go?

POPE
Who go?

GIRL
My brother.

POPE
I thought you were he.

GIRL
I am a girl.

POPE
You must be twins.

GIRL
Others have noticed a resemblance.

POPE
What is your name, child?

GIRL
Perdita.

POPE
Oh, dear. I seem to remember that name.
(SHEPHERD BOY enters)
POPE
There you are.

PERDITA
Ulysses!

SHEPHERD
That is not my name.

POPE
(To PERDITA)
Are you sure you have the right one?

PERDITA
No. But I think if the name fits.

SHEPHERD
I am called Candide, Candy for short.

POPE
Now I know why everyone liked you so much.

CANDY
I thought they all hated me.

POPE
Same thing.

PERDITA
You gave them indigestion.

POPE
Worse.

PERDITA
Where are we?

CANDY
We are looking for a red person.

PERDITA
But where are we?

POPE
Someone said this was Purgatory.

PERDITA
What? It can't be. I'm not dead.

CANDY
That's what you think.

POPE
We are looking for a dead Cardinal.

PERDITA
A bird? In the Outer Hebrides? I mean, Purgatory?

POPE
Who told you about the Outer Hebrides?

PERDITA
It just looked familiar.

POPE
Have you been here before?

PERDITA
I come from here, like my brother.

POPE
Oh.

PERDITA
Anyway, I have seen a man dressed in red.

POPE
With horns?

CANDY
And a forked tail?

POPE
He carries a large fork.
(PERDITA looks confused)

CANDY
To spear souls. He eats them. On the run.

PERDITA
We are all on the run.

POPE
It is time to make a stand.

CANDY
Yes. I am tired of running.

PERDITA
Me, too.

POPE
Then we must find the Cardinal that killed me. Avant!
(The CARDINAL appears upstage, then runs off)

PERDITA
Was that him?

POPE
I didn't have my glasses on.

CANDY
He looked familiar.

POPE
They all look the same.

CANDY
Very conservative.

POPE
Backward looking.

PERDITA
I try always to look progressive. That is where the future lies.

POPE
Our future is stretching before us.

CANDY
What about the Cardinal?

POPE
He's not going anywhere.

PERDITA
We are – we are conquering ourselves, and that is a step in the right direction.

CANDY
You mean there is a way out of Purgatory?

POPE
There has to be.
(CANDY starts to cry)

CANDY
I didn't choose to be a catamite.

POPE
I am so sorry.

PERDITA
I didn't choose to die.

CANDY
Don't tell us. It will give me the horrors.

PERDITA
You already have the horrors.
(The POPE, CANDY, and PERDITA are all silent)

CANDY
I am afraid.

POPE
I feel a bit peppy.

PERDITA
A bright future can change your day.

POPE
How old are you?

CANDY
She's fourteen.

POPE
(To CANDY)
And you?

PERDITA
Nineteen.

POPE
Then you can't be twins.

PERDITA
Then we are an optical illusion.

POPE
Maybe I am hallucinating.

CANDY
I don't think so.
(The POPE looks dazed)

PERDITA
You are a former Pope. No wonder you are confused.

POPE
I am your superior, and I am not confused.

PERDITA
Yes, you are. You think you aren't, but you are. Very confused.

POPE
I have never in my life been confused.

PERDITA
You are not alive, and you have always been confused. Now that you are dead, *(indicating herself and Candy)* we are going to reform you. That is why we are here. Then all three of us can get out of Purgatory.

(The POPE is silent)

POPE
Where do you propose to begin?

PERDITA
With the Cardinal.

CANDY
And my sheep.

POPE
Sheep, sheep, can you think of anything else?

CANDY
It is better than thinking of you.

PERDITA
Stop! Be constructive. Mr. Pope, you are dead and, therefore, superior to no one. It is just like being mad in a madhouse. There are no social grades here. We are not a cast society.

POPE
But this is an exclusive neighborhood!

CANDY
Think again.

POPE
You mean I have to listen to the wisdom of a fourteen-year-old girl?

CANDY
(To POPE)
What do you know? What brought you here? Your experience can't be too deep, nor your knowledge.

POPE
Death is deep.

PERDITA
Death is what you make of it, just like life. It looks to me like you have failed in both.
(The POPE is astounded)

POPE
Now look here, if you are going to lecture me, I will sic that Cardinal on you.

PERDITA
Nonsense. He's just like you, only worse. I am not afraid of either of you. All you can do now is mock me, and mocking is an empty weapon.

POPE
Dear Lord, preserve me from young girls.

CANDY
I thought He had. Where is He anyway?
(GODOT enters with full cast except CARDINAL)

GODOT
Do I have a voice?
(To PERDITA)
And who are you?

PERDITA

A dead duck.

POPE

Duckling.

PERDITA

He just dislikes me because I am a girl and smarter and prettier than him.

GODOT

(To POPE)

Have you been abusing people again?

POPE

People?

GODOT

A poor Shepherd without sheep and his sister.

POPE

They abuse me.

PERDITA

We are trying to educate him to the realities of death, and he is being unrealistic.

POPE

(To PERDITA)

What do you know?

GODOT

(To POPE)

Quiet!

(To PERDITA)

The truth sometimes has to be approached obliquely, as though you were trying to catch a wild cat.

PERDITA
Can we tame him?
(Everyone looks dubious)

GODOT
That is my stock-in-trade.

POPE
Youth is cruel – it has certainly been cruel to me.

PERDITA
Age has its limits.

GODOT
Providence has brought us together. Let us find out why.
(The CARDINAL enters with choker around his neck and chain dragging behind him)

GODOT
Ah! *Le Nouveau Venu.*

CARDINAL
Please don't accuse me of social climbing.

POPE
(With venom.)
You do not do yourself justice.

GODOT
(To POPE)
Wait your turn, please.

POPE
But he killed me, with his own heart. Blackguard! He was a *poseur* and ingratiated himself. I trusted him.
(POPE begins to cry)

CARDINAL
It is your own fault. You are a fool. You take yourself too seriously.

POPE
Beast!

GODOT
A little quiet, please.

CARDINAL
It was a secret decision of the College of Cardinals. His wrongs and insufficiencies were too great to tolerate. It is all your own fault. It was the only way out we could devise.

GODOT
If you two do not stop, I will send you back to life.

POPE
You!?

CARDINAL
You!?

UNCLE STURTEVANT
All we need is a little love.
(Everyone astounded, looks at him)

LADY DALY
(To STURTEVANT)
What are you, a weak reed?

DOTTIE
You look a bit dusty. Would you like to be cleaned?

LUCILLE
How about a stiff gin?

ALICE
I could serve you something. Today's special is tongue with raspberries and orange sauce.

LANCELOT
I could analyze. *Pro bono.*

LADY DALY
Pro bono publico.

DANIEL
I could offer them my innocence.

GODOT
You're too late.

POPE
It's never too late to say goodbye.
(POPE does not move)

GODOT
Your slip is showing.
(POPE searches his raiment. He brings out a rabbit)

POPE
(Perplexed)
Where did that come from?

PERDITA
Dinner.

GODOT
We don't eat here.

POPE
Then why is it here?

CARDINAL
You ought to know.

POPE
I know nothing.

CARDINAL
At last, the truth.

POPE
You have all set me up.

DOTTIE
He doesn't look like a Rabbit.

LADY DALY
Looks aren't everything.

LANCELOT
There are more –

LADY DALY
Where that came from.
(POPE pulls out a frog)

LUCILLE
Haute cuisine.

ALICE
Frog legs.
(POPE pulls out a dinner bell. He rings it)

GODOT
Yes, flesh is perishable.

LADY DALY
And edible.

GODOT
Here, we do not eat.

DOTTIE
They will make nice pets.
(They all look at POPE and CARDINAL)

POPE
I am not a pet.
(CARDINAL takes off choker and chain)

CARDINAL
Me, neither.

LANCELOT
Let us drive them into each other's arms.
(POPE and CARDINAL back away from each other)

DANIEL
The repulsion of the same.

GODOT
We are achieving something.
(POPE and CARDINAL embrace)

DANIEL
The laws of physics have been reversed.

GODOT
No. We are just seeing the final conjugation of evil.

POPE
What?

CARDINAL
What?

DOTTIE
I think they are going to Hades.

GODOT
We call it Hell. They love each other. They created it on earth, now they can enjoy their time together permanently.

POPE
(To GODOT)
You are an imposter.

GODOT
You are the imposter. And your Cardinal is only a pale shadow of yourself.

CARDINAL
We are not afraid of you.

GODOT
We are not afraid of you. Take off those clothes.

CARDINAL
(Embraces POPE)
It is too cold.

GODOT
You will not miss what you haven't earned. Take them off.
(CARDINAL drops cape and miter)

GODOT
(To POPE)
Your turn.
(POPE follows suit)

GODOT
Now you can love each other as it suits you.
(POPE and CARDINAL look at each other, first in disbelief, then with growing aversion)

GODOT
(To DANIEL)
Tie them together. They have created their own permanent bond.

LUCILLE
(To POPE and CARDINAL)
May I offer you a sloe gin?
(POPE and CARDINAL drink glass of gin like water)

LUCILLE
That was quick.
(LUCILLE refills their glasses. They drink again, this time savoring their drinks)

LUCILLE
Take your time.
(LUCILLE refills glasses. She hands Pope her bottle of gin)

LUCILLE
We have more.
(POPE and CARDINAL begin to laugh)
GODOT
What a couple.
DOTTIE
Very sweet.
GODOT
They have found themselves.
DANIEL
They have found each other.
LANCELOT
A light love for a dark pair.
ALICE
I can take care of them.
GODOT
Let them take care of each other. We have to prepare for the next wave. I see a lot of red rising in the distance.
DANIEL
We get the whole College of Cardinals?
GODOT
Rome has exploded.
(Everyone is surprised)
GODOT
Metaphorically, of course. But I do anticipate some more company.
DANIEL
Where are they all going to sleep?

GODOT
With their souls.

DANIEL
Alone?

GODOT
I should think so.

DANIEL
What about the sheep?

CANDY
Now they are free.

DANIEL
You found them?

CANDY
I have let them go for good.

DANIEL
For good?

GODOT
Very good.

CANDY
Now Perdita and I can go home.

PERDITA
We are home.

GODOT
Join us, if you like.

CANDY
Now that my sheep are free, so am I.

PERDITA
And me.

GODOT
You have all been arrested. Now you are free.

DANIEL
What about those two?

LUCILLE
They have found each other.

DANIEL
They can't see.

GODOT
Right.

LUCILLE
Do they have a future?

GODOT
That is still to be seen. Some choices flow in one direction only, like time.

DANIEL
You mean they are tied together for eternity.

GODOT
Unless they choose nothing. That is their only hope.

DOTTIE
Hope?

LADY DALY
I would call that hope forlorn.

GODOT
For them it is the sole way out.

DANIEL
Dear Godot.

LANCELOT
When does the red stampede hit us?

GODOT
They will take their time. First, they must make up their minds what to do.

DANIEL
Do they know how to choose?

GODOT
As well as I or you.

DANIEL
I see fire in your eyes.

GODOT
They will ask me to give you up.

DANIEL
But we love each other.

GODOT
That is why they want me to give you up.

DANIEL
Can't we share our love with everyone?

GODOT
It is possible.

DANIEL
Will they permit it?

GODOT
Look.
(POPE and CARDINAL, tied together, try to walk)
(POPE and CARDINAL manage to hop offstage)

LANCELOT
Imagine that!
(LANCELOT looks in disbelief at the retreating couple)

ACT III

SCENE 2

Scene opens with entire cast seated around DANIEL, CANDY, PERDITA, and GODOT, officiating. PERDITA is dressed as for marriage, and stands between the other two young men.

GODOT
Are we ready?

PERDITA
Oh, Mr. Godot, I am frightened.

CANDY
I am too young to get married.

DANIEL
I am too old.

GODOT
First, pretend it is the rehearsal, and everything will be fine. Now, Perdita, do you take Candy and Daniel in the civil bond of love?

PERDITA
I suppose so.

GODOT
Please.

PERDITA

Yes.

GODOT

And you, Daniel, and Candy, do you both take Perdita in the civil bond of love?

CANDY

Yes.

DANIEL

Yes.

GODOT

And Candy, do you take Daniel as your love?

CANDY

Yes.

GODOT

And, Daniel, do you take Candy in love?

DANIEL

Isn't he a little young?

CANDY

Nonsense.

GODOT

His experience makes up for his youth. Daniel?

DANIEL

I do.

GODOT

Now all three of you may kiss each other.
(They do)

DANIEL

(To GODOT)
I still love you.

GODOT
That is alright. Just be willing to share me with the rest of the world.

DANIEL
Dead or alive?

GODOT
At this point, the dead outnumber the living; after all, the Universe have been around longer than Earth, and individuals have been passing away for a good part of that time.

DANIEL
Then the Universe is full of other souls?

GODOT
Anywhere you care to go.

UNCLE STURTEVANT
I don't see too many here.

GODOT
Oh no, Uncle. You are a select group.

UNCLE STURTEVANT
When do we join the others?

GODOT
Whenever you wish.

UNCLE STURTEVANT
What?

GODOT
There is a cliff looking out over the sea just a bit south of here. When you are ready, you jump off.

UNCLE STURTEVANT
I cannot fly.

GODOT
You will not. You will not lose yourself, only your body. The rest of you will be translated elsewhere.

UNCLE STURTEVANT
And where is elsewhere?

CAST
Yes?

GODOT
The realm of spirit.

DANIEL
That sounds rather vague.

CANDY
Don't we three get some Honeymoon first?

PERDITA
If we jump off your cliff, we won't be able to consummate our union.

CANDY
Not even in triplicate.

DANIEL
No.

GODOT
You may enjoy each other here for as long as you like.

LADY DALY
They won't last.
(DANIEL, PERDITA, and CANDY look disappointed)

GODOT
I assure you, the further realm of the spirit is far beyond what you can experience here.

LUCILLE
I rather like cocktails.

DOTTIE
Spirits don't collect dust.

LANCELOT
There are no mad people in the beyond.

GODOT
I am afraid your current identities will not extend to the sphere of the beyond.

ALICE
And I thought nobility, even without a title, might be permanent.

GODOT
As I say, you needn't jump until you are ready.

DOTTIE
I don't want to.

GODOT
The present is always becoming the future.

UNCLE STURTEVANT
And vice versa.

GODOT
Yes. And the future is as long as you may wish. When you are tired of Existence, you may get out.

LUCILLE
Opt out?

GODOT
Yes. You may return to Nothing out of which you were born.

DANIEL
What is Nothing?

GODOT
The only truth that can be said about Nothing is that it does not exist.

DANIEL
Then, ultimately, all we face is Nothing.

GODOT
Right.

LADY DALY
Left.

DANIEL
And in between.

UNCLE STURTEVANT
Then why are we here?

GODOT
Anyone?

(All silent)

GODOT
To pass the time. As you wish. Time is the secret of choice, and choice is what you do as long as you enjoy life or death, one form of existence or another.

LANCELOT
Then in the end, it is all the same what we do.

GODOT
Not at all. Your existence has its peculiar shape. That shape is what you choose.

UNCLE STURTEVANT
Can't we abstain?

DOTTIE
I don't want to choose.

GODOT
That is your choice.

LUCILLE
Oh, dear. I think I need a drink.

GODOT
That is your choice.

LADY DALY
I ain't jumpin' off no cliff. That's my choice.

GODOT
Suit yourself. Some day you will tire of all this, and that is the day you will become spirit and realize yourself. Until then, you will merely be a shadow floating on the shore of the Outer Hebrides.

(Godot begins to wrap his garments around him. He slowly rises off the ground. Lights settle on him, shadows engulf the others)

GODOT
I must leave you now.

DANIEL
Dear Mr. Godot, where are you going?

GODOT
Everywhere and nowhere. My destiny was sealed at birth. So was yours. Now, I must visit other people in other worlds. The Universe is vast, and almost all of it lies beyond your comprehension, and even your imagination.

DOTTIE
Oh, Mr. Godot, don't go.

LADY DALY AND OTHERS
Don't leave us. What will happen to us without you?
(GODOT is already gone)

- END -

CODA

GODOT
The life of the heart is almost as difficult as the life of the mind.

DANIEL
Moreso. I know. I have a heart.

GODOT
I do, too. For you.

DOTTIE
What about me?

GODOT
For all of you. But I am particularly attached to Daniel.

UNCLE STURTEVANT
I thought you had to be impartial, that you had to treat us all equally.

GODOT
My mistake.

LADY DALY
It was no mistake. Anyone my color knows that.

GODOT
I am doomed.

DANIEL
Not at all. You have our love, love from all of us.

GODOT
Great.

LUCILLE
Are you going to belittle us?
(GODOT assumes tired air)
GODOT
My problems are immense – and universal. Love, love, everywhere you look you fall into a trap. I have gotten tired of the whole set-up. I arranged the possibilities. It was your choice what to do.
LADY DALY
We have heard this before.
UNCLE STURTEVANT
It gets us nowhere.
GODOT
On the contrary, it assures your future.
DANIEL
If we are dead, we don't have a future.
GODOT
If you are dead, that is all you have.
LUCILLE
What about our past?
GODOT
You possess that, too.
DANIEL
So we have memory and anticipation.
GODOT
You can always opt out.
DANIEL
How?

GODOT
Follow the Pope and confine yourself to the eternal present.

ALICE
This is too much for me. I am only a waitress.

GODOT
I am only Godot.

DANIEL
Don't be such a pushover.

UNCLE STURTEVANT
Someone has to tell us what to do!
(Dottie breaks into tears)

GODOT
Let me think. What if I say that you have entered the Great School of Trial and Error?

UNCLE STURTEVANT
You try, we err.

GODOT
I, too, am allowed to err.

DANIEL
How do you know when you are in error?

GODOT
I watch your faces. I listen to your heart. I feel your breath upon my lips and sometimes, late at night, when the whole world is asleep, I cry tears down. That is when I know we are all alive. And we are all alone: even here, together in the Outer Hebrides. Life is a simple puzzle, and once it breaks, you must face the future. I am here to help.

DOTTIE
And we help you, as much as we can.

GODOT
Thank you, Dottie. Thank you all. You have given me your love, and I fear I can only love you back.

LUCILLE
Only?

ALICE
Only?

GODOT
Where does my love get you?

LUCILLE
You have given us back our confidence.

ALICE
You have allowed us to assume our new and real identity.

UNCLE STURTEVANT
You have touched us so that we can never forget.

DANIEL
You have taken away our pain.

LADY DALY
You have made me strong.

LANCELOT
You have weakened my false power, so that I can use it in a new shape for new purposes.

LADY DALY
Love is very powerful, Mr. Godot. Even yours has power. And you must not let yourself think that your mission here or anywhere else is inconsequential. You have found us, you have changed what you found, and we will always be in your debt. So we owe you our future, dead or alive, and we are glad of it. What else could we ask for?

DANIEL
Oh, Mr. Godot, you have helped so much!

LUCILLE
Is there a cocktail in the house?

GODOT
Lucille, I will have a stiff gin martini.

DOTTIE
Champagne for the homeless and unoccupied!

ALICE
(Serving champagne)
Now I am occupied.

DANIEL
Let us all be occupied with something.

UNCLE STURTEVANT
Life – and Death – present us with a great opportunity.

LUCILLE
I want to live!

GODOT
So do I. And I think I can do it with you – through you, and you through me!
(All form a circle around Godot and toast him)

GODOT
Now I must leave you again. Do not forget me.

DANIEL
I cannot.

LADY DALY
Nor I.

DOTTIE
Nor I.

GODOT
Dear Dottie, you remind me of myself in my youth.

DANIEL
Oh, Mr. Godot, were you ever young?

GODOT
I am older than those hills, and once I had a history. And before that –

DANIEL
The night was everywhere.

DOTTIE
Now we are somewhere.

ALICE
And each one of us is someone.

GODOT
I hope in my absence you will take care of one another. I have, indeed, set you up. Now you may proceed on your own.
(POPE and CARDINAL enter)

GODOT
You may begin by giving those two a little instruction.
(GODOT rises out of sight)
(Lights shine on POPE and CARDINAL in rags, still chained to each other)
(BLACKOUT)

-FINIS-

The President Pardons Godot

༄

A Comedy

CAST OF CHARACTERS

A AND B: The Two Apostates

MADAME GODOT: Wife of Godot

GODOT: Himself

DANIEL: Son of A, B, Madame, and Godot

PRESIDENT (aka JACK): The former President of the United States

LANCELOT BROWN: Psychiatrist, then President

LADY DALY: His wife and former patient (Later: Aide 1)

DOTTIE: Patient (Later: Aide 2)

LUCILLE: Patient

ALICE: Patient

UNCLE STURTEVANT: Patient

DR. FISH: Resident in Vermont

LIZ: Daniel's girlfriend

ANTONIO: Bartender

ACT I

SCENE 1

A desolate wasteland near the Outer Hebrides.

    A
Did he ever beat you?

    B
Beat me? I beat myself. Everyday.

    A
It's a pleasure?

    B
Yes.

    A
Can you teach me?

    B
We don't have time.

    A
I thought we had eternity.

    B
We are waiting on a tea date.

    A
A what?

B
We have invited someone to tea.

A
Here?

B
It will help us get along.

B
Who's coming?
(B looks upstage to northern horizon)

B
I see her now!

A
Who?

B
Our guest. Madame Godot.

A
Madame?

B
The wife of our friend.

A
That one…

B
His wife.

A
And she's coming now?
(MADAME enters)

B
Bonjour, Madame.

MADAME
Enchanted.

A
Me, too.

B
And me.

A
Should we speak French?

MADAME
I speak English.

A
Thank Heavens.

MADAME
You must be American.

A
(To MADAME GODOT)
Can I call you Ma'am? This is not France.

MADAME
You can call me anything you like. Most names will fit, and almost every history.

A
We must get to know you better.

MADAME
That is why I am here.

B
What about your husband, Godot?

MADAME
He is dressing.

          B
Oh.

          A
Getting ready for his entrance?

          MADAME
Not at all. He dresses to please himself, and sometimes the result is spectacular.

          B
Yes.

          A
We know.

          A
(Continuing to B)
I could have told you.

          B
(To MADAME)
I have met your husband.

          MADAME
Many people have, only they don't know it.

          B
He is a bit of a jongleur.

          A
What?

          B
Magician. I rather like it when he levitates.
(To MADAME)
Maybe he could teach us…

          MADAME
I'll pass on the request.

B
We don't want to presume...

A
Oh, no.

MADAME
No problem. He'd be delighted to teach someone something. After all these years, I am certain he would welcome you as pupils.

A
I make a good pupil. I always did well at school, especially in kindergarten.

B
What did you do in kindergarten?

A
Slept, mostly.

MADAME
Dreams are fun.

B
Yes.

A
I remember closing my eyes very tight and seeing a large red ball of light.

B
And then the light went out.

A
I met you.

B
You opened your eyes.

A
You opened my eyes.

B
I am trying.
(Turns to MADAME)
Have you ever seen the sunrise in the Outer Hebrides?

MADAME
This is the first time I have come here.

A
We hope to see more of you.

B
It's not so bad.
(The earth shakes. MADAME looks alarmed)

A
Just a little earthquake. To liven up eternity.
(B frowns at A)

MADAME
I didn't know the earth could shift here.

A
It does everywhere, sooner or later, but here it's pretty minimal.

B
Just enough to open your eyes.

A
Make you gasp. Not much is going on, otherwise.
(There is another shake)

B
Where is Godot?

A
Yes.

MADAME
He should arrive in a moment.

A
(Quietly to B)
Isn't she a bit stiff?

B
(Quietly to A)
She's French.

A
Ah. Bien entendu.

B
Madame, do you have any children?

MADAME
(Astonished)
Too many, I think.

A
(To B)
We are prime suspects.

B
(To MADAME)
Then all humanity?
(MADAME nods)

B
Oh.

A
It's no good being a Unitarian any more.

B
Do you recommend one religion over another?

MADAME
You should ask my husband. He leads, at least he leads me.

B
Then you are not a feminist?

MADAME
Not yet.

A
Even with a husband?

B
(To A)
You have me.

A
Ah.
(DANIEL enters)

B
Here comes our own child.

DANIEL
(To MADAME)
I am Daniel.

MADAME
You are one of my favorite children.

DANIEL
But A and B are my parents.

B
By adoption.

DANIEL
Then…

A
It looks like it.

DANIEL
Where have you been?

MADAME
I am a working mother.

A
She hasn't been working on you.

B
Here's your chance.

MADAME
Daniel, I am, in fact, your mother.

DANIEL
Then who is my father?
(GODOT enters)

GODOT
Hello.
(Everyone freezes. DANIEL looks crushed)

DANIEL
You're my father?
(GODOT smiles)

DANIEL
What about our affair?

GODOT
Love is almost as varied as creation.

A
This is beginning to sound like the Greeks.

DANIEL
So you cast yourself as Zeus?

MADAME
He is not Zeus, and I am not Hera.

DANIEL
Do I have to share you with her?

A
Is that your only problem?
(There is a silence)

MADAME
In any case, I do not mind. Daniel loves his father, and that is correct.

DANIEL
At least we haven't slept together.

MADAME
Why not? I doubt you two could produce any children.

B
(Hinting)
What about the taboo?

GODOT
Taboo?

A
Incest?

MADAME
Many people are far more familiar with my husband than that.

GODOT
They eat me for dessert.

A
They don't seem to know it.

B
Should we consider ourselves pantheists?

GODOT

Consider yourselves whatever you like. The facts are the facts. And Daniel is our son. As for our affair, it has gone up and down, like everything else in these matters. I believe we have been intimate, and there were no unfortunate results. In fact, our intimacy confirmed our love. And I don't know that your taboo applies to the relation between two males.

B

Perhaps we should resurrect Socrates and get him to examine the subject.

A

It's a new one.

GODOT

I don't see anything new in it.

DANIEL

You don't?

GODOT

You know who I am. Everyone here is my child, even my wife. For me, your taboo is either universal or irrelevant. I prefer to think the latter, at least when I am with you.

(DANIEL feels a little better)

GODOT

Anyway, there is no reason to quarrel.

A

It's a family quarrel.

GODOT

I suppose.

DANIEL

But what about us?

MADAME
What about me? Have you no love left for your mother?

DANIEL
But this is the first time I have ever met you.

GODOT
You'll just have to get to know each other.

DANIEL
But I have never loved a woman.
(A, B, and GODOT raise eyebrows)

MADAME
Here I am.

DANIEL
I am not Oedipus.

GODOT
And I am not Socrates. Your mother loves you particularly, just as I do, and if you don't want to sleep with her, that shows good judgment. You are nevertheless entitled - encouraged - to love her as your mother. Once you get to know her, you will see.

MADAME
Are men and women so different that you cannot love both?
(DANIEL is at a loss)

B
Life is hard. I recommend you get a job. It will take your mind off all this and maybe even let you redirect your attention to a nice girl your own age.
(DANIEL sputters)

A
Girls aren't that awful.

DANIEL
How do you know?
(B nudges A)

DANIEL
Well?

B
I think life offers us all many possibilities. It is up to you to look at them. Not one of us is entirely like any other, so we will not try to force you to do anything against your own nature.

A
But we do encourage you to explore.

DANIEL
After Godot, what comes next?
(GODOT and MADAME smile)

GODOT
It is your task to find out.

MADAME
And we will encourage you to do so.
(DANIEL looks a little disappointed)

A
Such is life.

B
Daniel, we are all here to help, though I suppose Godot and his wife have a great deal of other things to think about.

GODOT
Daniel, your mother and I are always here to accept your love, and we return it.

MADAME
Where is our tea?

GODOT
Tea?

MADAME
We were invited to tea.

A
That's my job. Come along. I'll get you your tea. It will settle the situation.

(They all exit stage right)

ACT I

SCENE 2 – THE TEA PARTY

Lights up on GODOT, MADAME, A, B, and DANIEL sitting around a low table covered with the paraphernalia of tea. They drink and converse alternately as the scene progresses.

GODOT
(Pouring)
Such good tea. What is it called?

A
Lapsang Souchong.

B
A bit smoky.

A
Our favorite

GODOT
It is very good.

MADAME
It reminds me of China.

GODOT
I almost died there once.

MADAME
It was during our visit in the sixties.

GODOT
I was very ill, and news got out that I had died.

MADAME
It created a sensation in America. Godot made the cover of Time.

GODOT
Then we moved on to Japan.

MADAME
The topography in Japan is smilier to this, at least in the north.

GODOT
We always seem to end up in the north.

MADAME
The Japanese reporters asked us about our health.

GODOT
I told them I was dead.
(GODOT and MADAME smile)

MADAME
Memories.

GODOT
Yes. The reporters were not amused.

MADAME
They were responsible for the story in the first place.

GODOT
I had the great pleasure of reading my own obituaries.

MADAME
He was amused.

GODOT
They were not accurate.

MADAME
Very flattering, but not accurate.

GODOT
These days people say the situation is reversed. Not only am I quite alive, some people say I am alive in the White House.
(Everyone laughs)
(A figure dressed like Abraham Lincoln appears in the shadows upstage behind the backs of the others)

GODOT
Yes, the White House.

DANIEL
Have you ever been in the White House?

GODOT
Only incognito.

MADAME
You see...

GODOT
I try not to interfere...

MADAME
He is aloof...

GODOT
I must maintain the possibility of freedom for everyone, so I do not interfere.

MADAME
He encourages.

GODOT
I try to set an example.

MADAME
He does not -

GODOT
I do not dictate.

MADAME
He wishes to encourage individual responsibility.

GODOT
Free choice.
(Black figure steps forward. It is the PRESIDENT)

PRESIDENT
Who are you?

GODOT
Who are you?

PRESIDENT
I am the President.

DANIEL
Of what?

PRESIDENT
The United States.

DANIEL
Of America?

PRESIDENT
Are there any others?

GODOT
Not yet.

MADAME
Would you care for some tea?

A
It is Lapsang Souchong.

B
From China.

MADAME
Yes. It is very good.

PRESIDENT
Decaffeinated?

A
Don't worry, it won't keep you awake.

B
(Making conversation)
Mr. President, what have you been doing lately?
(PRESIDENT is silent)

MADAME
Milk?
(PRESIDENT nods)

MADAME
Sugar?
(PRESIDENT signals no)

PRESIDENT
I do love sweets, but my doctors have taken me off them.

GODOT
Too bad.

PRESIDENT
Thank you.

MADAME
The milk is nice.

B
So, how does it go in Washington?

A
Comme ci, comme ça?

PRESIDENT
We are at war.

MADAME
There is always a war somewhere.
(Pointing to teacups)
Which one is yours?

PRESIDENT
It is not my war. The enemy brought it on themselves.

MADAME
They always do. It is so tiresome.

PRESIDENT
Try being President.

GODOT
I once knew a President who was on perpetual vacation. He played at being President. He enjoyed it.
(There is a silence)

GODOT
He even played at war, when he was not playing golf.
(The PRESIDENT is visibly stiffening)

MADAME
I am certain you are a more serious President than that one, n'est-ce pas, Mr. President?

PRESIDENT
Who are you people, and what am I doing here?

GODOT
I think you are out of office.

B
Something happened.

MADAME
I should have introduced us. I am Madame Godot, this is my husband, Monsieur Godot, then we have A and B
(A and B nod)
and their adoptive son, Daniel.

PRESIDENT
Out of office?

GODOT
Shall I tell him?

DANIEL
You are dead. We are all dead.

PRESIDENT
Nonsense. What is this place?

MADAME
Be civil. And you are dead.

GODOT
You are in the Outer Hebrides.

PRESIDENT
Where are my aides?

MADAME
Isn't it obvious?

GODOT
They are alive. You are not.

PRESIDENT
This is unbearable. I want my aides.
(Tea drinkers raise their eyebrows)

GODOT
Don't you know?

PRESIDENT
Know what?

GODOT
You have been assassinated.

PRESIDENT
You are all crazy. How do I get out of here?

DANIEL
I can show you a way out.

GODOT
There is a cliff a little south of here...

PRESIDENT
(Breaking down)
Am I really dead?

MADAME
That's what the newspapers say.

PRESIDENT
But they only print what they hear from me.

GODOT
The Truth.

B
From you and your aides, too.
(PRESIDENT closes his eyes, then opens them)

GODOT
It is not a dream and you are still here.

PRESIDENT
How do I get back?

DANIEL
You like golf that much?

PRESIDENT
Well, it's the thing everyone… who are you?

DANIEL
Daniel. Adopted and not.

A
(Whispering to B)
Maybe we should adopt the President.

B
(To PRESIDENT)
Would you like us to adopt you?

PRESIDENT
What for?

GODOT
We could teach you how to play golf without walking.

DANIEL
We could give you quite a ride.

A
I used to play golf, and this is Scotland.

B
Maybe we could arrange something, a game with professionals.

A
There are many specialists up here in the Outer Hebrides.

PRESIDENT
I hate golf.
(There is silence)

MADAME
More milk?

GODOT
More tea?

PRESIDENT
I don't much care for tea.

GODOT
We knew that.

MADAME
Here, we drink tea all the time.

GODOT
Anywhere we go: China, Japan.

A
The Outer Hebrides.

PRESIDENT
I can't be dead.
(There is silence)

PRESIDENT
Who killed me?
(There is silence)

PRESIDENT
Who...

GODOT
Your daughters.

PRESIDENT
That is lunacy. I told them never to visit me in the White House.

DANIEL
What about the ranch?

PRESIDENT
The ranch? I think I remember something.

(Everyone begins to smile, except the PRESIDENT who is cogitating)

GODOT
(Quietly)
Let him think.

PRESIDENT
I think I remember an accident.

B
It was not an accident.

PRESIDENT
But where are my daughters?

MADAME
What does it matter? They are there…

B
…and you are here.

A
With us.

GODOT
Have some more tea.

MADAME
Tea has symbolic value: it stands for Truth.

PRESIDENT
Oh.

MADAME
Would you care for some more?

PRESIDENT
Truth?

GODOT
It's a little dicey, isn't it?
(PRESIDENT is silent)

PRESIDENT
How much money do you want?
(Everyone laughs, except the PRESIDENT)

GODOT
People are always offering me things.

B
Money…

DANIEL
Youth…

MADAME
Labor…

A
Attention…

GODOT
Prayers…

PRESIDENT
How much? I have a lot.

GODOT
Mr. President, look into your soul. Do you see any money there?

DANIEL
Now you are pure soul, like the rest of us.

MADAME
Have some more tea.

GODOT
Soul can be very expensive.

(Pausing)
It can cost you your life.

A
B and I discovered our souls before we died.

B
Then we didn't need much money.

A
And here we are.

B
With you.

GODOT
In the Outer Hebrides.

MADAME
With you.

PRESIDENT
I'll give you anything you want. You can be Secretary of State.
(There is silence)

PRESIDENT
I'll recommend you as my successor.
(There is big silence)

GODOT
I don't think I want anything from you, Mr. President, except, perhaps, the truth.
(The PRESIDENT is getting really desperate)

PRESIDENT
Mr. Godot, I pardon you. I pardon all of you.

GODOT
We do not need your pardon, Mr. President. We have done nothing wrong.

MADAME
We would like to pardon you, Mr. President.

A
Just for form's sake, Mr. President.

B
As a matter of course.

A
Even though we are all dead.

B
It hardly makes any difference now.

A
To the world.

B
Yes, to the world.

A
But we still have our future time together to consider.

B
Yes.

GODOT
So we pardon you, too, Mr. President.

MADAME
And we thank you for taking such good care of us.

GODOT
Consult your soul, Mr. President. What do you really want?

PRESIDENT
I want to go home.
(PRESIDENT breaks down in tears)

GODOT
I have heard that so many times, mostly from the mad.

MADAME
All those psychiatric wards, full of pain.

GODOT
They only wanted to go home.

MADAME
And there was no home.

GODOT
No.

A
No.

B
No.

DANIEL
No.

MADAME
(Brightly)
And now we are here.

PRESIDENT
You say my daughters killed me? How could they? I loved them.

GODOT
Mr. President, you are very green.

B
Very fit for a tragedy.

GODOT
And now you have had your tragedy.

B
And you can't take it.

GODOT
You will. You will learn.

MADAME
We all learn.

DANIEL
We all learn.

A
We all suffer, one side of life or the other.

GODOT
Death is a great teacher. Very powerful. More powerful than you, Mr. President.

MADAME
How many people have you killed, Mr. President, I mean besides yourself?

PRESIDENT
But I didn't kill myself.

GODOT
Yes, you did. You may think you didn't, but you did.
(PRESIDENT gets up and begins to walk away)

DANIEL
Where are you going, Mr. President?
(PRESIDENT moves a bit further away)

PRESIDENT
If this is death, you are welcome to it. I am going home. To Washington. I am the President. I must find my aides. I am at war. I am responsible. I am the most powerful man on the face of the earth. My daughters love me. My wife is waiting for me. Always.

GODOT
Yes. You are the Defender of Freedom. Wherever you go. Well,

don't let us stop you. You may walk back to Washington.

MADAME
The long way round.

DANIEL
You can start by acquiring an education. Like me. There is always time to get an education.

MADAME
We all have oodles of time.

GODOT
Why in a rush, Mr. President? If you go back, you will find that time has left you behind. No one wants you back. They have moved on.

DANIEL
Now it is your turn to move on, Mr. President.

MADAME
May we call you "Jack?" "Mr. President" is so cumbersome – and out of date.

GODOT
It no longer applies.

A
Let bygones go by.

PRESIDENT
I feel very tired.
(PRESIDENT tries to sit on the ground)

PRESIDENT
Do you have an extra chair? Jack?

DANIEL
Take mine. I can stand.

GODOT
(Smiling)
I'm sure you can.
(To PRESIDENT)
Please. You are our guest.

PRESIDENT
May I have some more tea?

MADAME
Of course.
(PRESIDENT sips tea)

PRESIDENT
It is hot.

GODOT
It always is, especially up here, we feel it, in the rain and wind, on the heath.

MADAME
If you will.

PRESIDENT
You call me Jack?

MADAME
Or "Jacques." We are diplomats, along with everything else, and French is still the language of diplomacy.

PRESIDENT
I'll take "Jack."

GODOT
Fine. How's your tea?

JACK
I've never had this before. What do you call it?

MADAME
"Lapsang Souchong." It comes from China.

JACK
It tastes of smoke.

MADAME
It is famous for that.

GODOT
It is famous for a lot of things.

DANIEL
So are all of us —

A
— Now.

B
Yes.

GODOT
Well, we have done our good deed of the day.

JACK
What are you all doing?

GODOT
You need some sleep.

A
Or at least a rest.

MADAME
Tea time can be very tiring.

A
All that conversation.
(JACK has already fallen asleep)
(Lights fade to penumbra. Actors freeze on stage)
(BLACKOUT)

ACT II

SCENE 1 – The President's Dream

We are back at the Budinger Foundation. There are chairs on stage arranged in a semicircle facing the audience, enough to seat everyone in the scene. At center of chairs sits the PRESIDENT, wrapped in a straightjacket. Each actor, when speaking, stands. Staff and Patients are indistinguishable from each other, though this appearance is not maintained when someone speaks.

DR. BROWN
(Banging on the floor to bring the meeting to order)
  Quiet, everyone! I being our community meeting today with sad news: My friend Mr. Godot was found drowned on the Isle of Palms near Charleston, South Carolina yesterday.

PRESIDENT
  Hooray! He was a troublemaker and a liberal. We had him under surveillance all through his phony convalescence.

DR. BROWN
  Please. Godot was a good man. Tortured by his dreams, but principled in any case.

LADY DALY
(Very downcast)
  It is too bad.

GODOT
Yes. I loved myself.

DOTTIE
He helped me with the dust.

PRESIDENT
Now he is dust, and …

DR. BROWN
… and you will be too if you don't be quiet, Mr. President.
(One of the Patients begins to throttle the PRESIDENT)

PRESIDENT
Help! I have no arms!

DR. BROWN
Get him off the President. We are not launching a revolution. This is a place of healing. I know you are all feeling down, but I know equally well you will one day feel much better, and then you will thank us for saving you.

PRESIDENT
Help!

DR. BROWN
Mr. President!

PRESIDENT
I want to go home!

GODOT
You are home.

LADY DALY
You can put your sausage you know where.

LUCILLE
Now, dears.

ALICE
Don't quibble over death. Suicide runs in the human race. Why, the twentieth century saw more butchering than the preceding ten centuries combined.

DOTTIE
What a mess.

DR. BROWN
But now we have been born again, and I hope I speak for the world in saying —

PRESIDENT
Vive le Quebec libre!

DR. BROWN
One more word, Mr. President, and we'll send you to the quiet room.
(PRESIDENT subsides)

DR. BROWN
Now, in memory of Godot…

GODOT
I want to say a prayer, in remembrance of myself —
"May the grace that
Gives life beauty,
And the love
That hallows it,
Be with us all."
(Everyone looks at GODOT)

ALICE
That was nice.

LUCILLE
Darling.
(DR. BROWN clears his throat)

DR. BROWN
Please. We know you are free of disease, as homosexuality is no longer a crime or even a mental disability. But be discreet. To continue: does anyone have anything to share with us today?

UNCLE STURTEVANT
When are we leaving?

DR. BROWN
When the world is ready for you.
(GODOT stands as if to speak, then sits perplexed)

DR. BROWN
Mr. Godot?

GODOT
If we are here, and the world is there, where am I?

PRESIDENT
A little lie might convince someone to let you out.

DR. BROWN
Mr. President, you interrupt too much and have nothing to say. Yesterday you smuggled in beer, got drunk and tried to rape a male nurse. This cannot continue.
(PRESIDENT smirks and ogles a handsome male intern)

ALICE
(To LUCILLE quietly)
How did he ever get elected?

LUCILLE
At least we are not promiscuous.

ALICE
I love you.

LUCILLE
I love you.
(PRESIDENT'S eyes begin to twitch)

DR. BROWN
(To nurse)
Get him some cogentin.

GODOT
He needs fresh air.

DOTTIE
He's too fresh as it is. He attacked me as soon as he arrived, and I am not young.

GODOT
Neither is he.

LUCILLE
He looks almost worn out.

ALICE
The job is big and he is small.
(PRESIDENT spreads his legs and screams)

PRESIDENT
Look at me!
(Everyone looks. PRESIDENT subsides)

DR. BROWN
Now...

PRESIDENT
(Interrupts)
The food here stinks.

LUCILLE
Mr. President, let's not be infantile. You will be here for a while and you will get used to it.

GODOT
I doubt it.
(PRESIDENT smirks again, then leers at everyone present)

DR. BROWN
I think that is all for today.
(BLACKOUT)

ACT II

SCENE 2 – The Outer Hebrides

        GODOT
Perhaps a little medication would help.
(PRESIDENT is writhing in his sleep on the ground)

        GODOT
Any suggestions?

        MADAME
Some more tea.

        A
Let's not overdose him.

        B
Reality is a great cure.

        GODOT
We have to bring him up gently.
(Quietly)
   Mr. President? Jack?
(PRESIDENT stops writhing)

        MADAME
Sir?

PRESIDENT
Yes?

MADAME
Are you awake?
(PRESIDENT looks around)

PRESIDENT
I thought I was mad.

A
You were.

B
Now you are saved.

PRESIDENT
How can you tell?

GODOT
Now you are awake.

MADAME
Did you have a pleasant rest?

PRESIDENT
I was in a straightjacket.

A
Really?

GODOT
Did it help?

PRESIDENT
Help?

DANIEL
It must have been a nightmare.

PRESIDENT
No worse than the White House.

DANIEL
You can get used to anything.

GODOT
Even the White House.

PRESIDENT
Am I alive?

GODOT
(With patience)
You are beyond life, and learning fast.

PRESIDENT
I don't want to learn. I know enough already.

MADAME
Of course, my dear. But don't you think a little change of mind would suit the change of scenery?

PRESIDENT
I can't change.

GODOT
You are already changing.

PRESIDENT
I don't want to change.

MADAME
That is because you love yourself too much.

B
You know what the Greeks said?

PRESIDENT
What Greeks?

B
(Slowly)
Gnothi sauton — know thyself.

PRESIDENT
How much is there to know?

GODOT
We will find out.

PRESIDENT
I don't want to know.

GODOT
Shall we put you to sleep again?
(PRESIDENT begins to shake)

B
I think he's entering recovery mode.

PRESIDENT
Recovery from what?

GODOT
Life.

A
It doesn't take long.

B
A and I have been working on it for the last two thousand years. It gave us something to do.

PRESIDENT
Two thousand years?

A
Approximately.

PRESIDENT
Maybe I am crazy.

GODOT
His mind is lifting.

        A
He is beginning to feel intelligent.

        PRESIDENT
I don't ever want to fall asleep again.

        A
(To GODOT)
Don't push things.

        GODOT
What difference does it make? He's an ex-President without a retinue.

        PRESIDENT
I am lost.

        A
You are found.

        GODOT
You are lucky to have found us.
(PRESIDENT groans)

        A
This guy will not move.

        B
Let's build a fire underneath him.

        MADAME
Mr. President, some tea with your entertainment?
(PRESIDENT groans)

        PRESIDENT
I need a drink.

        GODOT
Brandy?
(GODOT offers a bottle. PRESIDENT takes a long drink)

A
He's retrogressing.

B
Maybe we should put him to sleep again.
(PRESIDENT drinks again)

GODOT
At this rate, he'll be soused before we finish the show. Mr. President...
(PRESIDENT leers)

PRESIDENT
Yes?

GODOT
Brandy is not beer. I'll take it back, now.

MADAME
He's in his cups again.

A
He was never out of them.

GODOT
Mr. President, are you prepared for a new life?

PRESIDENT
I don't want to go back.

GODOT
Not back, forward.

PRESIDENT
They were all hurting me, and I didn't know it.

A
You were tough.

PRESIDENT
(Drinking)
I still am.

GODOT
I am powerless.

B
Where is Dr. Fish?

A
He went back to Vermont.

B
That's a help.
(DR. FISH enters)

DR. FISH
Here I am!

GODOT
I cannot seem to cure this one. It is the only failure of my life.
(Grand silence)

GODOT
Yes. Well, Dr. Fish, do you have a new idea?

FISH
Ignore him.

PRESIDENT
What?
(Everyone ignores this)

GODOT
A fast life can lead you to a terrifying end.

MADAME
Tea has always restored me.

PRESIDENT
Hello! Is anyone listening to me?
(PRESIDENT jumps up and down)

GODOT
Even our dreams can sometimes defeat us.

A
Look at the world.

PRESIDENT
Look at me!

A
Don't look at the world.

MADAME
I have some Earl Grey today.
(DANIEL enters)

DANIEL
Hello.

PRESIDENT
I know you.
(GODOT takes DANIEL aside)

GODOT
Just ignore him.
(To MADAME)
Earl Grey? I thought titles were on their way out.

A
They are.

B
And so are the people who hold them.

GODOT
People keep calling me Lord.

MADAME
It's redundant.

GODOT
I am no Lord, nor a Prince, nor a King of anything. I do not wrap myself in velvet and silk, nor eat off gold; nor do I live in a palace.

(GODOT gestures to the surrounding air)

GODOT
I am here with you. You are my children, and I love you, all of you.

MADAME
Have some tea.

GODOT
Thank you.

DANIEL
Mr. Godot...

(A very beautiful young woman enters and waves to DANIEL. Everyone looks at her and then to DANIEL, then they pause)

DANIEL
I have met someone new.

PRESIDENT
Road kill?

(PRESIDENT is ignored)

DANIEL
(To everyone)
Her name is Elizabeth.

LIZ
"Liz."

MADAME
I approve already.

GODOT
I have gained a daughter.

A
This is a surprise.
(To B)
I wonder if he will still love us.

B
Daniel, we bless you.

GODOT
And Liz.

MADAME
She is very beautiful.

PRESIDENT
But can she talk?

LIZ
Who is that person?

DANIEL
It doesn't matter. Mr. Godot, is it alright if I...

GODOT
Daniel, as I have already said, love has many faces.

MADAME
We will always love you.

GODOT
Yes.

A & B
We will, too.

PRESIDENT
Doesn't anyone love me?
(They all ignore him)

MADAME
Some kinds of love come cheap.

PRESIDENT
I am not cheap!
(Everyone ignores this)

DANIEL
I am glad you like Liz.

LIZ
I like your friends. I can usually judge someone by the friends they keep.

A
(To B)
She's smart, too.

B
Double lovely.

LIZ
But why so many men here?

DANIEL
It looks as though I have three fathers, and only one mother.

A
He was adopted.

B
We adopted him.

GODOT
I conceived him.

MADAME
I bore him.

DANIEL
And here I am, surrounded by love.

PRESIDENT
It will not get you anywhere!
(PRESIDENT gets up, then slips and falls into a mud puddle. Everyone continues to ignore him)

PRESIDENT
Help! Help! Help!

MADAME
Rather windy today.

GODOT
Quite a breeze.

A
I could use a nice piece of toast.

B
I need a gin and tonic.

GODOT
(Brandishing a bottle)
Brandy, anyone?
(GODOT distributes glasses and pours)

PRESIDENT
Won't anyone listen to me?
(They all continue to ignore PRESIDENT)

MADAME
(To DANIEL)
Have you read Wind In the Willows recently?

DANIEL
I never liked that one. All those talking animals.

GODOT
What about "Doctor Doolittle?"

A
My doctors never did much for me.

B
Doctors... Dentists are the worst. I think those x-rays must have been what brought on the cancer.

PRESIDENT
(Desperately)
Cancer?

MADAME
We all die, even of cancer.

GODOT
Some of us die of presumption.

B
Some of us die of other people's presumption.

PRESIDENT
Look at me!
(All continue to studiously ignore him)

LIZ
How is life in the Outer Hebrides? I have never been here before.

A
You will get used to it.

B
(Quietly)
Should I tell her?

DANIEL
That is my job. Liz, you are dead. All of us are dead.

LIZ

Things seem the same. You feel solid. I can smell your hair. Your lips are keen to kiss. And there is a lot more of you that I hope to explore.

DANIEL

You will. But we are dead.

LIZ

Then I guess we don't need to get married. The economic question has been solved.

DANIEL

In more ways than you might think.

PRESIDENT

I will make you Secretary of the Treasury. I can make you all anything I want!

DANIEL

Liz, death offers you all the things life didn't: even love.

LIZ

I died for love.

GODOT

Don't go into that now, dear. There is plenty of time later to swap histories.

DANIEL

I am not interested in your history, Liz, only your present and our future.

A

Now he's gushing.

B

Love.

PRESIDENT
I am not gushing.
(The PRESIDENT is beginning to go mad)
PRESIDENT
I never gush. I love my aides. I love everyone. And the whole world loves me back. I am giving them all their freedom. That is the best I can do, as President.

MADAME
We seem to have run out of tea.

B
Anyone for coffee?

MADAME
But coffee is the drink of death.

A
Yes.

GODOT
Let us offer some to the President. Jack! You want something to drink?

PRESIDENT
(Slobbering)
Coffee? It will keep me awake.

GODOT
We don't want to interfere with your dreams.

MADAME
Any of them…

B
Have a nice cup of coffee. It will put you to sleep.

MADAME
He has put many people to sleep.

GODOT
It goes with the job.

DANIEL
Not at all. His predecessor fought wars without firing a shot.

GODOT
I knew him.
(There is silence)

GODOT
Ah, well. We are all human.

PRESIDENT
Reckless sinner!
(Everyone raises their eyebrows)

MADAME
Coffee, tea or milk?

A
Do you have anything solid to offer?

MADAME
We have a few stale scones. I made them myself.
(A tries one)

A
Very stale.

GODOT
I have told you, food is unnecessary here.

MADAME
But it still ranks as a superfluous pleasure.

PRESIDENT
Where is my pleasure?

GODOT
I wish Professor Fish were here. He would give us the right diagnosis.

B
I think he is depressed - and rapidly descending into paranoia.

MADAME
Maybe a little conversational therapy.

GODOT
He must help himself: that is the Conservative doctrine.

A
The Conservatives can be so doctrinaire.

B
And contradictory.

A
And hypocritical.

GODOT
Take the President -

PRESIDENT
Don't take me anywhere!

GODOT
You see. He has suddenly found his home.

MADAME
But he is mad.

GODOT
He was mad. Now he is waking up - to tea.

MADAME
Here.
(PRESIDENT cringes)

GODOT
Do not touch him yet. He is very sensitive.

A
I wonder if he made scenes like this in the White House?

          B
Probably.

          A
There he got away with it.

          B
He was President.

       PRESIDENT
Now I am dead.

        GODOT
I told you so.

       PRESIDENT
Who?

        GODOT
The others didn't think I could salvage you.

       PRESIDENT
Salvage?

        GODOT
All souls are equal, once they die. So I knew I could help. You were just carrying a lot of baggage.

       PRESIDENT
I can carry my own baggage.

        GODOT
That's a start.

          A
Start?

          B
Quiet!

       PRESIDENT
I will write you all into my will.

A
He's relapsing.

GODOT
As I said, this one is going to require unusual effort.

A
Look! A snake!
(PRESIDENT screams)

B
Where do we go now?

A
Uphill and down dale.

MADAME
Recoveries can take ages. It all depends on what you eat. Or drink.

PRESIDENT
Potato chips and a hamburger!

MADAME
At least he enjoys thinking about food.

GODOT
It will only give him the trots.

A
That is another start.

GODOT
You are beginning to understand my methods.

B
This is cruel.

GODOT
It is the only way I have discovered to squeeze out the evil in such people. It is hardly anything when compared to the pains they have brought to others.

A
I guess I am just soft on sin.

B
You are a Democrat.

A
And Godot is...?

B
I think Godot is realistic.

GODOT
My methods have so far worked with everyone you know.

B
We know.

A
I am still a Democrat.

B
I don't think Godot is either a Democrat or a Republican.
(GODOT smiles)

GODOT
You are all my children.

A
I once heard the Archbishop of Canterbury say that.

B
He had children?

A
He said, "We are all God's children."

B
Godot's.

A
Godot's.

GODOT
Yes. That particular Archbishop hadn't heard of me.

A
Now he has.

B
Now they all have.

A
Even us, in the Outer Hebrides.

B
What a joy!

A
(To GODOT)
You do offer us some comfort.
(A begins to cry. PRESIDENT begins to wail)

B
So this is how it goes. How long is he (pointing to President) going to take?

GODOT
I don't know. The wound is pretty deep.

MADAME
There is a lot of rot inside.

GODOT
I cannot use my usual tools. I think another dream might help.

A
We weren't privy to the last one.

GODOT
I was, in one of my many capacities.

B
You were in his dream?

GODOT
It helps if you pay attention to the patient.

A
Whoa!

B
So they call him Godot...

A
Let's watch the dream.
(*Lights dim. Two screens descend again. More speeches, scenes of war, etc. We are in the Oval Office. AIDES 1 and 2, DOTTIE and LADY DALY come in and out*)

AIDE 1
Where is the President?

AIDE 2
Powdering his nose.

AIDE 1
We have orders for the War.

AIDE 2
The usual.

AIDE 1
The usual war?

AIDE 2
Shh. He's coming.
(*Enter current President – LANCELOT BROWN*)

BROWN
What's on the menu?

AIDE 1
More signatures. Orders for the War.

BROWN
How many casualties today - on our side?

AIDE 2
Two.

BROWN
The usual. Where do I sign?
(BROWN signs)

PRESIDENT
But it's my war! I want it back!

GODOT
Be quiet. They can't hear you.

BROWN
What's for lunch?

AIDE 2
Health care.

BROWN
I'm not joking.

AIDE 1
I'll go see.
(AIDE 1 exits. BROWN studies ceiling)

AIDE 2
Fine day.

BROWN
I am playing golf this afternoon.
(Pausing)
With my contributors. Suckers.

AIDE 2
Yes sir.

AIDE 1
Choice of veal stew or meatloaf.

BROWN
Anything in the stew?

AIDE 1
I'll ask.
(AIDE 1 exits)

BROWN
Fine day.

AIDE 2
Very fine.

BROWN
It's a little boring here today. Shall we cook up another war? Protect the homeland? Get those creeps?

AIDE 2
Sir?

BROWN
I shoot very high. One war down, another to go.

AIDE 2
Yessir.

BROWN
Do you shoot?

AIDE 2
Excuse me, Sir?

BROWN
Do you hunt? Game?

AIDE 2
Game? A game?

BROWN
You know, deer, bear, elk?

AIDE 2
I haven't tried it, Sir. My husband would object.

BROWN
Great sport. Hunting them down.

AIDE 2
People?

BROWN
Animals. People are animals.

AIDE 2
Animals are people. Or so my daughter tells me.

BROWN
I didn't know you had one.

AIDE 2
One daughter.

BROWN
How old is she?

AIDE 2
Eight.

BROWN
Eight?

AIDE 2
Going to be nine in three days.

BROWN
Children...
(AIDE 1 re-enters)

AIDE 1

The stew is veal à l'Ancienne, with onions, mushrooms and Béchamel sauce.

BROWN

I'll have the meatloaf. My wife calls me pedestrian.

AIDE 1

Yessir.

AIDE 2

Yessir.

BROWN

Nonsense. She's just joking. Very pedestrian.

AIDE 1

Yes, Mr. President.

(PRESIDENT still is shadows next to GODOT)

PRESIDENT

I am usurped.

GODOT

They can't hear you.

PRESIDENT

Look at me!

(The others are oblivious)

GODOT

They don't remember you.

(PRESIDENT emits strangled sound)

BROWN

Life is hard. So much work.

(BROWN takes an apple off a desk and begins to eat it)

BROWN

So, what's next?

AIDE 1
It's one of your free days, Mr. President.

BROWN
I'll go work out.

AIDE 1
Yessir.

AIDE 2
Yessir.
(BROWN and AIDES exit)

PRESIDENT
No one listens any more.

GODOT
I am listening.

PRESIDENT
Could we talk?
(GODOT sits behind desk)

GODOT
(Getting up)
This is your place.

PRESIDENT
I resign.

GODOT
I accept.

PRESIDENT
Is this all that's left?

GODOT
An empty chair. An empty room.

PRESIDENT
They didn't even see me…

GODOT
They never will again.

PRESIDENT
But I still see myself.

GODOT
Now you do.
(PRESIDENT begins to cry)

GODOT
Tissue?
(GODOT hands PRESIDENT a hanky)

PRESIDENT
Thank you.

GODOT
A small favor for a big man.

PRESIDENT
But I'm not big anymore.

GODOT
You have just begun to be big.

PRESIDENT
But what can I do if I'm dead? I have no influence. They don't even know I'm here.

GODOT
Let's go back to your new friends. They may have an idea what to do.
(GODOT takes PRESIDENT by the shoulder and gently guides him out the door)
(SLOW FADE)

ACT III

SCENE 1

LADY DALY enters with PRESIDENT.

LADY DALY
We would like to help you, if we could.

PRESIDENT
But we're all dead.

GODOT
A small problem.

A
What do dead people do?

GODOT
Some say the good ones become angels.

DOTTIE
But we are all good, now that we are cured.

PRESIDENT
Cured of life...

GODOT
Yes. And so the ranks of angels are always growing.

A
But what do we do?

GODOT
You may stay here in the Outer Hebrides and drink tea, or you may jump off my famous cliff and authorize yourselves for another journey, or you may decamp to any part of the world and adopt a new role in life.

PRESIDENT
The transmigration of souls.

A
Where did he pick up that one?

B
Knowledge blooms in Godot's company.

A
So does love.

LADY DALY
I heard that.

GODOT
You are all correct. But you must make your choices, and the present is certainly a good time to begin —

PRESIDENT
— Again.

LADY DALY
(To PRESIDENT)
You have seen us in the White House.

PRESIDENT
Wasn't my replacement your husband?

LADY DALY
He was my husband. Now he's my boss.

A
Flip-flop.

GODOT
He was ready for the job.

PRESIDENT
This is extraordinary. But if Mr. Brown has taken my place, how do I get back?

GODOT
There are many roles in the world, as many as there are people. You can cast yourself however you wish, but you cannot come back as your former self. Can you think of anything that would interest you?

PRESIDENT
I've already been top man. How about Minister Plenipotentiary?

GODOT
How about Private Counselor?

PRESIDENT
I get no publicity? Where's the fun in that?

GODOT
That's where all the fun is. Trust me. It's my job.

PRESIDENT
Will you come with me?

GODOT
I'm a trouper, and I will be happy to help.

PRESDIENT
When do we begin? What do I wear?

GODOT
We begin as soon as possible. You ought to know what to wear.

PRESIDENT
I'll wear my favorite blue suit and my Hermes red tie.

GODOT
A little free publicity can always be helpful, as long as the product merits the praise.

PRESIDENT
Oooh, ooh. I'm excited.

GODOT
Don't get too excited. The world is a big mess. In your previous incarnation, you chose some ruinous policies.

PRESIDENT
I had to get re-elected.

GODOT
We all have to get re-elected, every day of our lives. Off with you!

(PRESIDENT and GODOT exit)

ACT III

SCENE 2

PRESIDENT
Doing nothing is very hard.
(Pausing)
I hope I can find something to do with eternity.

GODOT
That is my problem exactly. What to do?

PRESIDENT
Any answers?

GODOT
Make friends. Influence people.

PRESIDENT
But that is what I have been doing.

GODOT
On the wrong side of the mirror. Reverse yourself. Turn your life — your death — around.

PRESIDENT
I don't understand.

GODOT
Think of life and death as an example of matter and anti-matter.

PRESIDENT

Anti-matter?

GODOT

In physics, half of reality is missing. That is anti-matter. Some people think of it as black matter — as though it were invisible. It is not invisible. It is perceptible. It is what drives poets and seers. Think of Nature. Think of the Greeks. Think of all the Gods and Heroes. Think of them. Think of them and where they have gone now.

PRESIDENT

Not here.

GODOT

Wrong. You will meet your peers here soon enough. And some have chosen to live in the world. Int he world you have just left.

PRESIDENT

It has left me.

GODOT

Yes.

PRESIDENT

So what do we do?

GODOT

What do we ever do?

PRESIDENT

Become catatonic?

GODOT

That is what happens when you begin to discover the half of reality that you never knew.

PRESIDENT

I know.

GODOT
That discovery is very dangerous, and many do not survive. Others end up living their lives in a kind of excruciating twilight — caught between two worlds and never able to choose between them.

PRESIDENT
Here I am.

GODOT
Yes, you are here. Some more tea?

PRESIDENT
Is all that's left talking in the Outer Hebrides?

GODOT
Of course not. Consider yourself a soul on a journey to an infinity number of new worlds.

PRESIDENT
Will I always be alone?

GODOT
No. You have already met some companions, if you want them. If not, there are many more. Death has been at work for an eternity.

PRESIDENT
You are smart.

GODOT
You don't believe me?

PRESIDENT
I take you on faith.

GODOT
I am giving you the facts, and you will know that very soon. In the meantime, you may accept what I say however you wish. As for faith, I am not a great fan of being foolish. Anything can

be accepted as faith — people accept whole lifetimes on faith, and look what happens! Faith is a crutch and it holds nothing up except ignorance. You may dress yourself in faith. I do not.

PRESIDENT
You mean —

GODOT
I, too, am faced with the problem.

PRESIDENT
Me, too.
(They smile and exchange a non-voluptuous kiss)

PRESIDENT
So there really is love in Heaven.

GODOT
You are still in the Outer Hebrides, and Heaven is everywhere, even on Earth.

PRESIDENT
What about sex?

GODOT
It is simply the embodiment of love. And sometimes love is confused with lust.

PRESIDENT
I was hoping for a little lust in the other life.

GODOT
You can have it.

PRESIDENT
Oh.

GODOT
People generally die old, and if they do, they don't have much further use for lust. Like various types of food, it offers pleasure, nothing more.

PRESIDENT
What about procreation?

GODOT
I shall have to save that for another time. I see someone coming.

ACT III

SCENE 3

  A
I smell smoke.

  B
It must be the tea.

  A
Something is burning.

  B
Your brain or mine?
(A sees GODOT and PRESIDENT)

  A
O! The culprits. Are you overheating?

  PRESIDENT
We were just conversing.

  A
Ah. Did the words stick?

  GODOT
Jack makes a fine student.

  PRESIDENT
It is my new role in life — in death.

B
We are moving.

PRESIDENT
Moving?

A
We think two thousand years on the heath are enough.

B
We are at a jumping-off point.

A
We have come to a conclusion.

B
We are tired of being alone together.

A
So we are going South.

PRESIDENT
South?

A
To the cliff.

PRESIDENT
After such a short acquaintance?

B
You are not the only President in the universe.

A
We are jumping off the famous cliff.

B
All we needed was a little courage.

A
After two thousand years, we have gathered all the courage we need, and now we are ready to proceed into the unknown.

                B
The next phase.

                GODOT
The illimitable…

                A
(To PRESIDENT)
Nice to meet you.

                B
Yes.

                GODOT
You need a witness.

                PRESIDENT
Maybe we should have a jumping-off party.

                GODOT
Good idea!

                B
We don't need company.

                A
No.

                PRESIDENT
Of course you do. We all hope to follow your example, sooner or later.

                A
Alright. But don't take too long preparing.

                B
We don't want to lose our resolve.

                A
Art lives on self-discovery, and the art of life does too.

B
We are about to discover ourselves anew.

A
I wish I had a horn. We need a little advertisement if we are going to have a party.

B
Here.

A
Where did that come from?

B
(Pointing to GODOT)
Ask him.
(GODOT smiles)

A
Semper paratus.

GODOT
In one of my many incarnations...

A
(Interrupting)
...yes, we know.
(He blows the horn. DOTTIE, LADY DALY, BROWN and the rest appear. Lights go down. Lights up at the edge of the cliff. The cast are all standing around as at a cocktail party, with drinks, hors d'oeuvres, etc. Everyone is chatting pleasantly)

LUCILLE
This is the best cocktail I have ever tasted.

ALICE
The bartender is over there. He arrived just yesterday.
(To BARTENDER)
Antonio! Antonio!
(BARTENDER comes over)

ALICE
Lucille says this is a fabulous drink.

LUCILLE
The best I ever tasted.

ALICE
She is an expert.

LUCILLE
A connoisseur.

ANTONIO
(Smiling)
It is my job.
(He bows formally and attends to the others)

DOTTIE
No dust here.

LADY DALY
Solid rock.

BROWN
Am I dead again?
(Pauses)
I rather enjoyed being President.

LADY DALY
A suicide bomber blew you up, along with the West Wing.

BROWN
I don't see the suicide bomber.

GODOT
I have reduced him to nothing.
(There is silence)

A
How do we know this is going to work?

B
We don't want to end up as nothing.

PRESIDENT
(Looking at GODOT)
I think you have to take what he says on faith.
(GODOT shrugs)

GODOT
I have told you what I know.

A
Oh.

B
Oh.

A
Well, I am prepared to jump in any case.

B
Two thousand years on the heath are enough.

A
Another cocktail?

B
Let's go.
(They shake hands and wave to the others. They approach the abyss, then jump. Everyone gasps. Two flashes of light shoot up into the sky. There is a tremendous clap of thunder. The light recedes)

DOTTIE
That was fun.

LADY DALY
I wonder if it hurts.

GODOT
Not at all. It is my preferred method of getting from one venue to the next. And now it is my turn.

(GODOT jumps. Everyone gasps)

   LUCILLE
That was novel.

   DOTTIE
Yes.

(All present begin to look at each other with the same idea in mind)

   DOTTIE
Are you ready?

(They all nod. All jump off the cliff. Fireworks ensue)

—FINIS—

Hot Potatoes

CAST OF CHARACTERS

TALLULAH: Tallulah Bankhead

FRANK: Her boyfriend

SCENE I

A kitchen in FRANK'S apartment, with all the accoutrements necessary for making potato pancakes: scrapers, knives, potatoes, onion, et cetera. As the scene begins we see TALLULAH stage right, dressed in evening clothes, apparently ready to go out for dinner. FRANK stands behind or alongside a kitchen counter happily working at his pancakes, paying little attention to TALLULAH.

TALLULAH
Darling, what's that you're doing?

FRANK
I'm peeling potatoes.

TALLULAH
For what? Are you on K.P.?

FRANK
K.P.?

TALLULAH
Yes. K.P. Kitchen Patrol. Weren't you ever in the army? I was.

FRANK
Coast Guard.

TALLULAH
They don't eat potatoes?

FRANK
They eat fish.

TALLULAH
I should have known. Why don't we go out to dinner?

FRANK
I want you to taste my potato pancakes. I'm using an old family recipe.

TALLULAH
Potato pancakes. Aren't they somewhat plebeian?

FRANK
They are delicious. You eat them with applesauce. Absolute Heaven.

TALLULAH
I'd rather go out. There is a very nice Chinese restaurant down the block. Their cold sesame noodles are out of sight.

FRANK
Not for me. Anyway I'm almost halfway through. I can't stop now. Would you like to help?

TALLULAH
I don't think so. My daddy never taught me how to cook.

FRANK
What about your mother?

TALLULAH
My mother was never in a kitchen in her life. She hated kitchens.

FRANK
Did she eat well?

TALLULAH
Eating killed her.

FRANK
Oh, really? How?

TALLULAH
She ate a bad oyster. Are there oysters in this potato recipe?

FRANK
Certainly not. Oysters and potatoes don't mix. And I'm not out to kill you. You are in for a rare culinary treat.

TALLULAH
I prefer Chinese.

FRANK
Now, now. If it doesn't turn out well, we can always go out.

TALLULAH
Well, dinner at home is romantic, isn't it?

FRANK
What are you doing? No tampering with the chef while he's working. Ouch. You're pinching me.

TALLULAH
I'm just trying to see if there is a real man behind that apron.

FRANK
Of course I'm a real man. Who says I'm not?

TALLULAH
Well, if you are, prove it. Give me a kiss.

FRANK
I can't give you a kiss. I have potato all over my hands. What are you doing? Watch out! You're going to ruin my recipe. I'll kick you out of the kitchen if you don't behave.

TALLULAH
Darling, I love you when you cook. I just want a little kiss. Maybe a bigger kiss. Yes. Right there. Oooh. Let's keep going.

FRANK
Not now. I'm still working on the potatoes. The onion comes next.

TALLULAH
Onion? You're putting onion into these things?

FRANK
It's delicious. You'll love it. When cooked, onion has a very pleasant and subtle flavor. Don't you think?

TALLULAH
Onion makes me cry.

FRANK
Oh, well, move off. Over there. Yes. That's good. You shouldn't smell it from there.

TALLULAH
But I don't want to be away from you. I want to be up close. Where I can see the color of your eyes, where I can taste your lips and smell your hay-scented hair. You are so attractive, I cannot control myself. Please put away the onion and let me come back. Please.

FRANK
Not yet. I'm almost through with it. There. Now we just mix them all together, add two egg yolks and one white. Mix, mix, mix. Et voilà. German potato pancake batter. At the ready.

TALLULAH
How do you cook them?

FRANK
The same way I cook you, my dear, I turn up the heat.

TALLULAH
Ohh. Another kiss. I shall die of frustration. Darling, let's skip dinner altogether. It is so boring. Sitting down separated by such a big table. I like your lap better.

FRANK
Nonsense. Maybe for dessert. Don't be disappointed. The night is not even begun. I shall finish off these pancakes, we shall eat our dinner, and then I shall relieve you of all the frustration you may feel. What do you think about that?

TALLULAH
Fix the potatoes.

FRANK
I am. I am.

TALLULAH
You are such a sneak. I have never seen anyone take so long to declare his intentions. That's what you're doing, isn't it?

FRANK
Well...

TALLULAH
Let me sit in your lap.

FRANK
I haven't finished.

TALLULAH
Oh, come off it.

FRANK
There. Now. A kiss. Ohh. that was a long one. Ohh. Deep throat.

TALLULAH
Ouch.

FRANK
Just a love bite.

TALLULAH
Well, don't take my ear off. Wait. Let me get my ear-rings off.

FRANK
I'm waiting.

TALLULAH
I have to get it off, if you're going to be biting me.

FRANK
I'll stop.

TALLULAH
But I don't want you to stop. It feels so delicious. Oh, that was a nice one. Is anything happening in the downstairs department?

FRANK
Yes.

TALLULAH
Oohh, look at that.

FRANK
My pancakes!

TALLULAH
What about them?

FRANK
They're burning.

TALLULAH
Burning?

FRANK
Yes. Quick. Get off. There. Oh. Well. I'll just have to make some more.

TALLULAH
Don't you have more batter?

FRANK
Yes.

TALLULAH
Well.

FRANK
I'll make some more. There. Now this time don't distract me.

TALLULAH
Distract you?

FRANK
Yes. I must concentrate on my cooking.

TALLULAH
Well, I'm cooking too, and I may boil over. Why in Hades name can't you forget about your frigging potatoes and have some fun with me? I don't make myself available to just anyone.

FRANK
Darling, I know. I wanted to please you with dinner.

TALLULAH
You did. But it's just begun.

FRANK
Really?

TALLULAH
Yes. Now let me back in your lap. There. Let's try one of those big kisses. Really big. Ohh. That is good. You learn faster than most men half your age. Shall we proceed?

FRANK
Proceed?

TALLULAH
You don't think we stop here, do you?

FRANK
No.

TALLULAH
Where's the bedroom?

FRANK
Through there. I'll turn the pancakes.

TALLULAH
The pancakes, the pancakes.

FRANK
I think they're ready. Darling? Are you coming?

TALLULAH
Yes.

FRANK
Dinner is ready.

TALLULAH
You're not kidding. The pancakes runneth over. Come on over here, honey. We can save the pancakes for Christmas. Now. Off with the shirt. Thank you. Ohh, what a lovely chest. I always have liked understated muscles. A hint of brawn.

FRANK
I'm glad you like me.

TALLULAH
I don't know about the rest of you, honey, but so far you've got an incredible bod.

FRANK
I guess we don't know each other very well.

TALLULAH
I think we can take care of that. Now. Your pants. There. Very, very good. I adore muscular thighs. I called my last lover thunder-thighs. He loved it. Oh, I suppose I shouldn't talk about my past right now. And you're wearing bikini briefs. Look at what's inside…
(LIGHTS DOWN)

-*FINIS*-

The Fix

Based on a story by James Thurber, as told to me
by Ed Gallagher

CAST OF CHARACTERS

THE PRESIDENT OF THE UNITED STATES: A not very imposing gentleman nearing fifty, somewhat resembling Thomas E. Dewey

LIEUTENANT BRIAN COOLE: A war veteran, possibly 45, earthy, a loutish rogue

ATTENDANTS

SCENE I

An elegant sitting room atop the Waldorf-Astoria. A small bar stands stage right bearing a profusion of bottles, none of them full. As the scene opens, we see COOLE, stage left, sitting on a red settee drinking. A voice is heard offstage right.

PRESIDENT
Where is he?

ATTENDANT
In the sitting room. Drinking.

PRESIDENT
Yes. What's his name?

ATTENDANT
Coole. Lieutenant Brian Coole.

PRESIDENT
This the door?

ATTENDANT
No sir, here.

PRESIDENT
Thank you.
(ATTENDANT can be heard going off. PRESIDENT enters sitting room. COOLE waves)

PRESIDENT
How do you do?

COOLE
Who the hell are you?

PRESIDENT
The President.

COOLE
Of what?

PRESIDENT
The President of the United States.

COOLE
This is fine gin. Comes from Calcutta. Ever been in Inja? Full of corpses. And flies. The flies eat the corpses. But they have good gin. It keeps your mind off the corpses. If you drink enough, it keeps the flies off you. Pickled. See? President of the United States?
(PRESIDENT is at a loss)

COOLE
I thought so. New York is a dandy town, full of layabouts and frauds. How do I know you're not a fraud?

PRESIDENT
But this is the Waldorf.

COOLE
Phooey. You find frauds high and low. You could easily be my putrefied brother-in-law from Peoria looking for a handout, only I don't have a brother-in-law from Peoria. Wanna drink?
(COOLE takes one himself)

PRESIDENT
Now, look, I am the President...

COOLE
You don't look like him. Anyway, if you're the President, who am I?

PRESDIENT
You're...

COOLE
Ooooh, you don't know who I am.

PRESIDENT
Your name begins with a C.

COOLE
With a little further prompting, you may escape hanging. I'm an Irishman, and my name is...

PRESIDENT
... Coole!

COOLE
Bravo! You get the Medal of Honor.

PRESIDENT
But...

COOLE
Yes, you're here to award it to me. Have a drink.

PRESIDENT
I think I will.

COOLE
Yes. I have been a brave soldier, and you are here to give me a medal.

PRESIDENT
(Taking a drink)
Thank you.

COOLE
To my medal.

PRESIDENT
Yes.

COOLE
Don't you come with a bodyguard?

PRESIDENT
In the outer hall.

COOLE
Then you really are the President?

PRESIDENT
Yes, I think so.

COOLE
Good. Always happy to make a new acquaintance. Do you smoke?

PRESIDENT
No.

COOLE
Do you mind?
(COOLE pulls out a large cigar)

PRESIDENT
No.

COOLE
You are kind.
(Lights up)
Well, what's up?
(The PRESIDENT looks blank)

COOLE
A President and no small talk? I thought that was your stock-in-trade. Would you like to hear a joke?
(Proceeding)
If a raven brings a black baby, and a stork brings a white baby, what brings no baby? Give up? A swallow. I'll bet you never heard that one in your life. I only just heard it yesterday from a lady friend.
(The PRESIDENT looks increasingly pained)

COOLE
(Continuing)
Great girl. Anyways, now it's your turn.

PRESIDENT
I don't tell jokes.

COOLE
C'mon, it doesn't have to be dirty, just funny. C'mon.

PRESIDENT
(Stiffly)
I never tell jokes.

COOLE
Suit yourself, Mr. President. A little humor at the top would be a good thing for the Country. A little laugh keeps the mind open and the soul free. Are you a Republican or a Democrat?

PRESIDENT
What difference does that make?

COOLE
You should know better than I.

PRESIDENT
God.

COOLE
He is neither a Republican nor a Democrat. Well, I suppose you are ecumenical in pol.itics, and a good thing, too. Broad minds are a scarce commodity. But I do think you could develop your sense of humor.

PRESIDENT
What are we giving you this Medal for?

COOLE
Oh, I shot a few jerries in the Second War, and then saved my men in Korea by shipping out God knows how many chinks on a hilltop. It was swell.

PRESIDENT
Are you retired?

COOLE
Yup.

PRESIDENT
Married?

COOLE
Nope.

PRESIDENT
Where do you live?

COOLE
Braintree.

PRESIDENT
Ahh.

COOLE
Beautiful town. I live with my sister. Great woman. Loves purple dressing gowns. Husband left her.

PRESIDENT
Too bad.

COOLE
Yes.

PRESIDENT
You seem to be happy here, there.

COOLE
Very.

PRESIDENT
Look. I'm the President and I think you should be civil.

COOLE
I'm as civil as you.

PRESIDENT
Oh, shut up and have another.

COOLE
Thank you. Ever been to Braintree?

PRESIDENT
Haven't had the pleasure.

COOLE
Delightful place. Full of factories. They make shoes. See?
(COOLE shows the PRESIDENT his shoes)

PRESIDENT
Very nice.

COOLE
Another drink?

PRESIDENT
Ohh…

COOLE
Here. Ever shot anybody?

PRESIDENT
I went hunting once.

COOLE
Yeah. Hit anything?

PRESIDENT
My foot.

COOLE
You're the President. How about people?

PRESIDENT
What?

COOLE
Ever hoot a human being?

PRESIDENT
Well…

COOLE
I can see you haven't. It would show if you had. Ever been in a war?

PRESIDENT
I make wars.

COOLE
A real politician. I'm a drinker. What's your name, Mr. President?

PRESIDENT
Charles.

COOLE
Shoot-em up Charlie. That's you. You send the likes of us out to die and hang medals on our corpses.

PRESIDENT
Would you prefer politics?

COOLE
Yes. Well. Another drink?

PRESIDENT
You're very kind, but no thank you. I must be going. When do we start the ceremony?

COOLE
Four o'clock, they say.

PRESIDENT
It's a quarter to.

COOLE
I'll see you downstairs.

PRESIDENT
Yes.
(PRESIDENT exits and meets two attendants in the hall)
PRESIDENT
Get rid of him, any way you can.
(ATTENDANTS enter sitting room and after a brief struggle, throw COOLE out the window)
(It is four o'clock in the Waldorf ballroom)
PRESIDENT
Ladies and Gentlemen, it saddens me to tell you that the recipient of today's honor cannot be here to receive it. I have only now been informed that Lieutenant Brian Coole has fallen to his death from his suite on the thirteenth floor of this hotel. Lieutenant Coole and I knew each other only for a short time, yet I can say that he was a true hero, both in modesty and accomplishment. He killed literally dozens of Germans, in the Second World War, and in one Korean engagement, fought off at least one hundred enemy soldiers with his bare knuckles. Yet he lived in recent years in the comparative quiet of Braintree, Massachusetts, noted for its charming colonial houses. We shall all miss our hero, and I hope that you will pray with me that his soul may rise on a straight flight heavenward. Thank you.

-FINIS-

The Keewaydin Plays

The Cow: Part 1 and Part 2
A Dream

The Cow: Part 1 and Part 2

CAST OF CHARACTERS

MERRILY
POPS
COW

PART 1

MERRILY
You don't need a whole cow. We are not pigs.

POPS
You cannot get milk from half a cow.

MERRILY
Yes you can—the back half. Everybody does it. It is routine

POPS
So you cut the poor beast in half? It will have only two legs to stand on while we milk.

MERRILY
That's all that most people stand on.

POPS
But the back half of a cow?

MERRILY
We will train it.

POPS
Good luck.

MERRILY
I am an experienced trainer. I have been standing on two legs almost since I was born.

POPS
What are the results?

MERRILY
Can't you tell?
(She stands on one leg and tries to look like a crane resting—and she succeeds very well)

POPS
Hurrah! How long can you go like that?

MERRILY
Five minutes. I just need time enough to make my point.

POPS
Oh.

MERRILY
Now, about the cow...

POPS
(COW appears)
Oh!

MERRILY
What a dainty cow!

POPS
Reminds me of my aunt Sarah Jerusha.

MERRILY
Who?

POPS
A relative.

MERRILY
You're related to a cow?

POPS
Yes.

MERRILY
Family trees are so complicated. Mine includes two orangutans.

POPS
So I see.

MERRILY
And on my mother's side we have lots of Footes.

POPS
Feet.

MERRILY
No. F-O-O-T-E-S.

POPS
Oh.
(Lights up pipe)

MERRILY
You're polluting the environment.

POPS
Only the immediate environment.

MERRILY
Well, at Keewaydin we like to set a good example. The production of smoke is not attractive or healthy. For anybody.

POPS
Thanks for the lecture.

MERRILY
(Having second thoughts)
I guess a pipe is alright. It has a wonderful aroma.
(POPS smiles)
And I know you don't inhale, so I won't complain. Besides, it makes you look like Santa Claus.

POPS
Camouflage.

MERRILY
May I try?
(She takes the pipe and puffs once. She immediately starts coughing violently)

POPS
You need experience. I am a good trainer. I have been smoking a pipe almost since I was born.

MERRILY
I shall stick to bubble gum.

POPS
It gives you sweet breath.

MERRILY
And rotten teeth.

POPS
Heavens! What you get from one hand, the other hand taketh away.

MERRILY
Lemonade is nice.

POPS
Not bad.

MERRILY
Fresh spring water.

POPS
Ahh!

MERRILY
A rainbow trout pan-broiled at dusk, with embers glowing below the smoke.

POPS
Splendid.

MERRILY
Sticky buns.

POPS
My favorite anytime.

MERRILY
We have much to be thankful for.

POPS
Besides ourselves.

MERRILY
Yes. Look at all those people.
(Gestures toward the audience)

POPS
I know. They are our friends.

MERRILY
We ARE lucky.

-FINIS-

PART 2

> MERRILY
> This cow has laid an egg!
>
> POPS
> Impossible.
>
> MERRILY
> Why not? Anyone can lay an egg—with practice.
>
> POPS
> Some do it without practice.
>
> MERRILY
> What do you do once the egg is laid?
>
> POPS
> Have it for breakfast.
>
> MERRILY
> This one's very big.
>
> POPS
> Have it for dinner. Invite guests.
>
> MERRILY
> It's been sitting around for weeks.
>
> POPS
> It smells gaseous.
>
> MERRILY
> Aha!
>
> POPS
> What?

MERRILY
If it is gaseous, we can blow it up on July 4th, which is very soon. It will make a wonderful spectacle.

POPS
Brilliant. Does your cow have any other hidden talents?

MERRILY
Oh, I don't know. Sometimes it loses a spot or two: they fall off.

POPS
Must be a Holstein. We can call it Spot.

MERRILY
It's a bit big to be called Spot. Spot is for dogs.

POPS
Do you see a dog around here?

(They look for a dog)

MERRILY
Well, Pops, what would you name our cow?

POPS
Spot won't do?

MERRILY
Nope.

POPS
Fido. That's Latin for Faith.

MERRILY
I give up.

POPS
OK, how about Gertrude?

MERRILY
Excellent. If I have any children, you get to be godfather.

POPS
Do we baptize the cow?

MERRILY
Here's some milk.
(The COW gets wet)

POPS
I hereby baptise you: Gertrude.
(The COW moos happily)

MERRILY
I knew we chose the right name.

POPS
Does it have relatives? I have some milk left.

MERRILY
Drink it for breakfast.

POPS
Milk and eggs.

MERRILY
One egg, and not fresh.

POPS
Look at the balloon!

MERRILY
It's my birthday.

POPS
Congratulations. You have now lasted as long as the Peloponnesian War.

MERRILY
I am not at all sure that that is a good thing.

POPS
Age is what you make of it.

MERRILY
So is Keewaydin.

POPS
Your cow is quite handsome.

MERRILY
She is young and full of milk.

POPS
Can we expect any more eggs?

MERRILY
Certainly not. Eggs are not predictable, especially when they are laid by someone you know.

POPS
They take you by surprise.

MERRILY
With most people, yes.

POPS
Yet there are some—

MERRILY
There are some you can smell a mile away.

POPS
I shall be prepared.

MERRILY
Good idea.

POPS
Life here is almost ideal.

MERRILY
The cow is perfection.

POPS
You too.

(Hugs her)
          MERRILY
(Turning to audience)
   What about our friends?
          POPS
(To audience)
   You too.

-FINIS-

A Dream

CAST OF CHARACTERS

ALFRED

BALDY

TOURIST GUIDE

ALFRED
Piracy?

BALDY
Pirates. I see them coming.
(Continuing)
In Tahiti?

ALFRED
We're in Tahiti?

BALDY
But that's the Battersea Power Station. We must be in London.

ALFRED
The Eiffel Tower!

BALDY
The Parthenon!

ALFRED
We must be dreaming!

BALDY
Or moving very fast.

ALFRED
Satellites move fast.

BALDY
Yes, I believe they can circle the earth quite quickly.

ALFRED
But we're not high up.

BALDY
Then it's all a dream.

ALFRED
I hope it doesn't end yet.

BALDY
Why?

ALFRED
Well, I've always wanted to see Beijing. The Chinese are a remarkable people—and their culture is the oldest living culture on earth.

BALDY
They are very fortunate. Think what history has taught them.

ALFRED
And poetry.
(BALDY looks doubtful)

BALDY
Do you know Chinese?

ALFRED
I know how to say hello.

BALDY
That's a start.

ALFRED
In Russian I can say Ya Vas Lublju.

BALDY
What does that mean?

ALFRED
I love you.

BALDY
Oooh — that will get you very far. Maybe you can use it in

China. I am sure they would understand.

ALFRED
The Chinese are wise. They certainly deserve as much as anyone else.

BALDY
Well, let's get this dream moved over there.
(They do)

ALFRED
The forbidden city?

BALDY
Beautiful.

ALFRED
Fascinating. I wonder if they have tours?

BALDY
In a dream, anything is possible.
(A tour guide appears)

MISS HONEYPOT
I am Miss Honeypot. And I am told you want a guide.

ALFRED
It would be helpful.

MISS HONEYPOT
Since you are having a dream, you may see whatever you wish.

ALFRED
Let me think. The Fort. Where did the Emperor put the Fort?

MISS HONEYPOT
Fort?

ALFRED
The loo, the WC.

MISS HONEYPOT
That is a very serious question. After all, the son of the Sun had to preserve his image.

BALDY
Like the Wizard of Oz.

ALFRED
Of course.

MISS HONEYPOT
Ah, here we are.

ALFRED
A bit small.

MISS HONEYPOT
So as to be inconspicuous.

BALDY
And easy to clean.

MISS HONEYPOT
Very important.

ALFRED
And the kitchens?

MISS HONEYPOT
Follow me.

ALFRED
Fabulous. I infer that the Emperor did not dine out. These arrangements are magnificent.

BALDY
They enjoyed their food.

MISS HONEYPOT
Yes. One of my ancestors was a beekeeper by appointment to the Imperial Court.

ALFRED
That explains your name?

MISS HONEYPOT
Yes.

ALFRED
What did they eat?

MISS HONEYPOT
Almost anything that could be cooked and would taste good without upsetting the digestion.

BALDY
They must have had a varied menu.

MISS HONEYPOT
Indeed.

ALFRED
I hear there was a court poet.

MISS HONEYPOT
Oh, yes. He was very popular, as he told the truth without anyone objecting.

BALDY
Impossible.

MISS HONEYPOT
Well, not everyone understood what he was saying.

BALDY
Not even the critics?

MISS HONEYPOT
They were somewhat obtuse — and they didn't like verse. It makes you think.

BALDY
Well some of us are on permanent vacation when it comes to thinking.

MISS HONEYPOT
Yes. Any other requests?

BALDY
The Fort and the Kitchen. We've seen the important stuff.

ALFRED
I would like to send a photo of the Throne Room back to camp.

BALDY
We don't have a throne room at camp.

ALFRED
We don't need one.

BALDY
Certainly not. Nature herself looks after us, and we take care of the rest without much interference from above.

MISS HONEYPOT
Sounds attractive.

ALFRED
Oh, it is a type of arrangement that is becoming increasingly fashionable, indeed popular all over the world.

MISS HONEY POT
Sensible.

ALFRED
Well it is only common sense, but some very famous people never had much common sense.

BALDY
No, but they had plenty of brains.

ALFRED
Yes, we try not to imitate them in every way.

MISS HONEYPOT
Well, that is good.

ALFRED
And where is the way out?

MISS HONEYPOT
Since this is a dream, you should close your eyes and tap your heels three times, and when you open your eyes, you will be at Keewaydin.

(They follow the instructions and wake up at camp)

-*FINIS*-